T0196481

# My Visions from Almighty God

Shahnoza Yuldasheva

WESTBOW
PRESS®
A DIVISION OF THOMAS NELSON
& ZONDERVAN

This book is a work of non-fiction. Unless otherwise noted, the author and the publisher make no explicit guarantees as to the accuracy of the information contained in this book and in some cases, names of people and places have been altered to protect their privacy.

WestBow Press books may be ordered through booksellers or by contacting:

WestBow Press
A Division of Thomas Nelson & Zondervan
1663 Liberty Drive
Bloomington, IN 47403
www.westbowpress.com
1 (866) 928-1240

Because of the dynamic nature of the Internet, any web addresses or links contained in this book may have changed since publication and may no longer be valid. The views expressed in this work are solely those of the author and do not necessarily reflect the views of the publisher, and the publisher hereby disclaims any responsibility for them.

Any people depicted in stock imagery provided by Thinkstock are models, and such images are being used for illustrative purposes only. Certain stock imagery © Thinkstock.

ISBN: 978-1-5127-6354-6 (sc)
ISBN: 978-1-5127-6355-3 (hc)
ISBN: 978-1-5127-6353-9 (e)

Library of Congress Control Number: 2016918630

Print information available on the last page.

WestBow Press rev. date: 11/04/2016

# My Visions from Almighty God

Dear Readers! My name is Shahnoza Yuldasheva. I want to write this book ""My Visions from Almighty God"" to share the events from my life.

I decided to write about my life and how I met the Most High God. I want to share the knowledge that I received from Almighty God; and to show the Glory and Power of the Most High God to other people, using my life.

I had a chance to hear the voice of the Most High God in my dreams. When the Most High God spoke with me in my Visions, I understood that Almighty God put a huge responsibility on me - to share His words to as many people, as I can reach. I understand that I am one of the very lucky women in this world. At the same time, I understand the huge responsibility that Almighty God had put on me, directing me through my Dreams. That is why, writing the book about God's promises became my Big Dream and the Huge Goal of my life. I am thankful to the Most High God for helping me to reach that goal in my life.

At the beginning, I was planning to share my dreams only with my children, so they would be able, in future, to share that information with their own children – my grandchildren. Then, one day Almighty God told me to share His Words and speak about His Glory, and Power with all other God's children, as many as I can reach.

I believe that every person in this World comes to live with a certain duty, given by Almighty God. I believe that many people live such life that proves the Existence of Real God, and the fact that God Loves people, and He tries to help people to be healthy, wealthy and happy. My life is happened to be one of the bright evidence of Existence of Real God.

I met the Most High God, when I was 22 years old. I call my God — God of Abraham, Isaac and Yaakov.

I was born in the family of Muslim people. From my childhood my Mother taught me to pray every night, cause I often had the nightmares. I used to pray every night before I went to sleep. Before praying, I used to wash my hands and my body in order not to make a sin. I used to wear only the clean dresses for praying.

But for some reasons, I was sure that Almighty God was very strict to me like to everybody else. I was told that God punishes everybody, who makes even the small mistakes. So, I was afraid of the Most High God very much, but nevertheless, I used to pray every day before sleeping. I never thought that God loved me, as I was not a perfect person. I had some negative features in my character. I used to feel myself so guilty in front of God. In my mind, Almighty God was angry with me all the time. But nevertheless, I felt a huge support from my God every day.

I used to hear the low voice, talking inside of my heart from my childhood. This voice used to give me the advices, which were for my good, if I listened to them. Very often, I did not pay attention to that voice and to those advices.

I need to emphasize that the Most High God spoke with me and directed me using my Dreams (Visions). I have never seen God or God's face, but I have heard His Voice in my Visions, when He spoke to me. That is why, I am writing that Book to share my Visions. I want to share God's Promises and Advices from my Dreams, since I believe these words of Almighty God concern to every person in this life.

At first, I did not know that all those Visions were from the Most High God. After I met Jesus Christ in my dream and I started reading the Bible, I understood that those Dreams were from my Heavenly Father - Almighty God.

The first time I saw the Dream from God, when I was in the second grade in Public School. In my Dream, I saw how an Angel picked me up from my body. That Angel did not have eyes and ears. The color of the Angel was grey, with a flat like a triangle face. The Angel had grey, big wings. When the Angel picked me up from my body, I saw my brother and my sister sleeping next to me, because we were sleeping in one room. I tried to scream, but I could not pronounce a sound. Then, the Angel started to whirl me in a circle. I got scared a lot and I closed my eyes. When I opened my eyes, I was in the green forest with the Weeping Willow trees and green grasses everywhere. I was inside of a house in that forest. I was sitting and crying, as I wanted to go home to my parents. I saw an old woman in that house. She was looking at me and she did not help me to go back home. Then, I saw a young man in a white suit. I did not know those two people at that time. Later, when I met my husband and his mother, I recognized that young man in the white suit was my future husband and that old woman was my future mother-in-law.

That is why, when I met my future husband for the first time, I knew that we would marry with him, as I recognized his face from my dream. I was 20 years old, when I first met my husband.

When I was studying at the second grade in a Public School, Almighty God already informed me and showed me my future husband and his mother. With that Vision God showed me that I would not be happy with my husband and his family, because I was crying in that dream, being in that house at the forest.

Before my marriage, I graduated the high school and I started to study at a College, receiving my undergraduate degree. I believe that I need to share that part of my life, when the Most

High God made a miracle in my life and He helped me to pass the exams at the college.

My parents could not pay for the tutors, who could prepare me for the introductory government exams at the college, where I applied. This college of foreign languages had three introductory government exams, which all the prospective students had to pass in order to enter and study in that college. Those three exams were very difficult. Most of my friends used to go to three different tutors for three subjects to be ready to pass those three government exams. My parents could not afford those tutors, but still I wanted to study at that college of foreign languages. I knew and I was sure that I would live abroad in my future. I understood that I had to learn the English Language. Most of the students at that college were from rich families.

My father told me not to apply to that college, since we did not have enough money to pay for the tutors and for the education at that college. The prospective students, who earned the high scores, would have the chance to have a free education, when the government would pay for their tuition. I told to my father that the Most High God would help me to pass those exams and to receive the high scores. I was sure that Almighty God would help me to earn the high scores and I would have a chance to study without paying for my tuition. All my relatives were laughing at me, since I was acting like a small and naive child.

Only my mother supported me in my choice. She helped me to buy some books, with the help of which I could prepare myself for those exams. I used to learn those books from the early morning starting 06:00 am till midnight 12:00 am every day. I had been learning those books very hard almost two months.

I used to pray once a day and I used to ask the Most High God not to let me be on the shame in front of those people, who were laughing at me, since I was trusting Almighty God more than on the facts and realities of my life. All my relatives were sure that I would never pass those exams and I would never study at that college, cause my parents were not rich enough. I trusted on Almighty God and on His help more than I trusted on anybody or anything in my life. I used to tell my father and other relatives that the Most High God would help me to get the high scores, since Almighty God was aware of my hardworking and studying, without having a rest.

I went to the exams and I came back with the confidence that the Most High God would bring the miracle in my life in spite of the truth and the facts of reality.

The results of the exams came after two weeks. My father went to the college to check the list of the students, who got the high scores at those exams. Among those students, he saw my name in that list. He called and told me the news, with the tears on his eyes. My father told me, he had been sure that I would never get the necessary scores to study, without paying for the tuition. My father and all my relatives were surprised, how the Most High God helped me to earn the free education at such prestigious college, without attending the tutors in my native country.

This was a huge miracle that Almighty God brought into my life. That particular day, one of our neighbors made a wedding party. God gave us the chance to celebrate our victory at the huge wedding party, where most of my relatives were invited. My relatives congratulated me on that huge wedding party of our neighbor. I told to my parents that the Most High God not only gave me the victory, but Almighty God gave us the chance to celebrate that event, among our relatives in a huge wedding party. I will never forget that part of my life.

One year later, my sister went to the same college and she applied to study in it. She could not attend tutors, as our parents could not pay for the tutors. My sister also was enrolled in that college, but she could not get the high scores at those three exams to study without paying for her tuition. My parents had to pay for her tuition. At least, my sister got enough scores to study there, since it was not easy to be enrolled at this particular college in our native country. Thanks to the Most High God for His help.

Later on, my brother married and his young family used to live in our big house together with us. My brother married with my aunt's daughter. So, his wife was our relative. In our country, we have such a rule and tradition, when a daughter-in-law has to live with her husband's family, I mean with her father-in-law, mother-in-law and other family members. She had to do all the work about the house for her husband's relatives (cooking, cleaning, doing the laundry etc.).

My brother's wife was in a very nice relation with my sister and me. Later on, when she used to see us attending our college, my brother's wife started to tell bad things about my sister and me. She started telling lies about my sister and me to our neighbors, relatives and friends. She used to say that we (my sister and me) never used to clean the house and we never did any work about the house. But in reality, we (my sister and me) used to do all the work about the house, where we lived.

The only thing, we did not have time to do was cooking the food for a lunch and dinner, because we (me and my sister) had to leave the house early in the morning at 7:00 a.m. to go to the college. We used to come back from the college by 4:00 p.m. We used to come back home hungry and we did not have time to cook the lunch and dinner.

My brother's wife used to tell very bad things about my sister and me to our neighbors. She told all our relatives that we never used to do any work about the house. I remembered, once we came from our college and there was a huge fight in our family. I saw my grandmother crying. My aunts came to our home. My

8

brother's wife was screaming at my mother, telling her that, we (my sister and me) did not tell her good morning that day. My mother told her that we left at 7:00 a.m. and we could not see her, since she used to wake up after 9 a.m. every day. My Mother did not allow my sister and me to talk back and to protect us. I left to my room and I used to cry a lot for such injustice. All our relatives believed to those lies, since they did not live in our house.

One day, I felt sleep crying after another quarrel that my brother's wife made. In my dream, two young men came to the bed, where I was sleeping. They were wearing white, long shirts and pants. The bright light was coming from them. I did not know, who they were that time. These two young men told me with the smile on their face: "Why are you crying so much? You should never be stressed or worried of anything in your life and you should never cry". I asked them to tell me the reason why I should not cry. I told them the events that had happened in our family and the reason, why I used to cry. These two men told me to look at the sky. I looked up and I saw a white house in the very high top of the sky. These two men told me: "you will live in the Heaven with Almighty God. This news should give you strength to live happily. Don't take everything from your life too close to your heart, because this life is temporary and Almighty God is on your side. The life in the Heaven will be forever. So, live happily during your journey in this life and don't forget about your future home in Heaven." They told me the White House with the huge, white door was the Heaven. I looked again up at the sky and I saw the white huge door and I heard the very pleasant song of worshiping the Most High God. This worship song was so peaceful and so pleasant to listen. These two men told me that this news should make me happy for the rest of my life. They said not to pay any attention to the problems of my life, since God - Creator of the Universe - would protect and take care of me all the time.

Later, I understood that those two men in white clothes were Almighty God's two Angels, telling me the message from my Heavenly Father. I believe, those messages from those two Angels of God belonged not only to me, but also to every child of Almighty God on this Earth. Amen.

When I woke up, I felt so peaceful and happy that there would be a justice in my life. I was very happy that Almighty God was taking care of my family and me. I was so peaceful that God was controlling every situation in my life. I became sure that the Most High God was my Vindicator for those lies against my sister, my mother and me. I stopped getting stressed after that Dream.

Later on, my brother's wife got pregnant and she told everybody that she went to a doctor, and the ultrasound results showed that she would give a birth to a baby boy.

One day, I felt asleep in the afternoon and I saw a dream. In my vision an old woman came and sat down next to my bed. This old women told me that, even though, my sister-in-law told everybody that she would give a birth to a baby boy, in reality she would have a baby girl. The old woman showed me this baby girl. I noticed the baby girl had almost the same face like my Mother's face. She mentioned that my sister-in-law was not telling the truth to us.

Then, the old woman told me not to listen to my relatives, who were stating that I would have unhappy future. She told me I would have such a wonderful life and future that every girl would dream about such kind of life. The old woman was telling the truth about my future, but at that time I could not know about it. All my relatives used to tell me, I would have very unhappy future, because I was not beautiful and my parents were not rich. I was brown skinned and skinny girl at that time. I did not know the reason, why my uncles and aunts used to say such things about my future. May be because of my sister-in-law, since she used to tell everybody negative things about me.

Then, the old woman told me to look at the curtains in my room and she said I would see everything she had mentioned earlier on that curtain. I looked at the curtain and I could not see anything. Then, I looked at that white curtain in my room for the second time. Suddenly, I started seeing the different scenes on that white curtains.

I saw a green field with plenty of white sheep, walking on the green grass. In the middle of that field, I saw a tall green tree. One man, wearing white clothes, was sitting under that tree, watching and taking care of those sheep.

Then, I saw the second scene on the curtains. I saw myself with a man, holding a baby boy with black and curly hair. I was sitting at the round, white table. The man had been standing behind me, holding that cute baby boy on his hands. The interesting thing about the second scene was the fact that all of us (the round and white table, me, the man with the baby boy) were standing on the air. We were not standing on the floor, but on the air. The table itself was on the air. There were many green and beautiful leaves around us, hanging down from the sky. The second scene was so beautiful.

Then, the old woman told me: "Did you see that all my words are true? You will live a happy, abundant, prosperous life that every person dreams about. Remember, every person would dream to have such life like yours. Listen! Never take too close to your heart every single thing that people are talking about your future and life. Rely only on God. God is Your Shepherd. God will bring all your dreams to come true."

She also informed me that I would know beforehand everything that would happen in my life, because the Most High God would direct my steps and Almighty God would tell me beforehand, what was going to happen in my life. The old woman gave me these wonderful messages from Almighty God.

I woke up so happy and surprised after that dream, and after hearing the old woman's words. I told my Vision to my Mother and grandmother. I even drew all the scenes of my Vision in the form of pictures. My mother did not pay an attention to that dream, but my grandmother said I was not like the others. My grandmother told me that the Most High God showed His Love to me with the help of my Vision.

After couple of months, my brother's wife gave birth to a baby girl. My mother and grandmother were very surprised, since I told them several months ago that my sister-in-law would give a birth to a baby girl, but not to a baby boy.

At that time, I did not know who was the man, sitting under the tree and taking care of many sheep. Later, I learnt from the Bible, the man had been Jesus Christ. The following parts from the Bible explain my dream:

Ezekiel 34:11. (New Living Translation)"For this is what the Sovereign LORD says: I myself will search and find my sheep.

Ezekiel 34:12. (New International Version) As a shepherd looks after his scattered flocks when he is with them, so will I look after my sheep. I will rescue them from all the places where they were scattered on a day of clouds and darkness.

Ezekiel 34:13. (New International Version) I will bring them out from the nations and gather them from the countries, and I will bring them into their own land. I will pasture them on the mountains of Israel, in the ravines and in all the settlements in the land.

Ezekiel 34:14. (New International Version) I will tend them in a good pasture, and the mountain heights of Israel will be their grazing land. There they will lie down in a good grazing land, and there they will feed in a rich pasture on the mountains of Israel.

Ezekiel 34:15. (New International Version) I myself will tend my sheep and have them lie down, declares the Sovereign LORD.

Later on, my life had changed. I graduated the college and I received my Master's degree in Education in my native country.

I got married. During those several years, I did not see any vision from the Most High God. I got married and I used to live with my husband's family - his mother, father, sisters and their children - in one house.

From my childhood, I always had a feeling inside of my heart that my happiness would end after my marriage. I could not explain that feeling, but I was sure that after my marriage, I would become very unhappy woman. Somebody used to tell those words inside of my heart from the time, when I was a teenager. That is why I used to run away from getting married.

In my native country, parents always try to marry their children between the age of 18 and 20 years old, and most of the time, people used to marry without being in love. Future husband and wife barely knew each other. They used to get married, because their parents decided to marry them. This tradition is still very important in my native country in our days and still most of the people follow this tradition.

My parents made me marry my husband, even though I told my father that I did not like him, when I had seen him for the first time. I told to my father I wanted to continue receiving my education in Great Britain, and I asked my father to help me with the payment of my education. But my father told me that his responsibility was to marry me and, if my husband agreed and allowed me to study abroad, only then, I would have a chance to continue my education abroad.

I had no other choice than to listen to my father. I got married and I started to live in a village with my husband's family. I understood that my husband would never allow me to study abroad. My husband even did not allow me to work as a teacher in my native country. My husband wanted me to stay at home, doing all the works about the house (cooking, cleaning, taking care of his sheep and bulls, and chickens in his house).

I had to forget about all my dreams and career. I had to stay at home in the village. My husband worked as a butcher in his own meat store. So, he had to leave the house early at 7:00 a.m. and he used to come back home late, close to 10 p.m. every day. I used to sit at home with my mother-in-law, sisters-in-law and my father-in-law. My life became so unhappy and lonely. I even did not feel that my husband loved me. My husband never told me that he loved me. Our life was like a job or responsibility. I knew that my family was not based on love.

When my husband used to come home from his work, my mother-in-law used to tell him that I did not do any work about the house. She used to do that, because I could not take care of his bulls. My husband's relatives did not like me, because I was very scared of the bulls and I did not take care of them. I used to do all the other works about the house, but my mother-in-law used to complain every day to my husband that I never helped her with cooking or cleaning. He started to believe to his mother's lie and he used to fight with me most of the time. He told me that I had to learn to take care of those bulls.

I was pregnant that time. I was really scared to go close to those bulls. So, my husband began being rude to me, screaming at me. I used to ask my husband to take me to my parent's place sometimes, for couple of hours, to have some fun with them at least. My parents lived in the city and they had the Internet, TV, and more fun than the place in the village, where I had been living. I lived without a TV and computer. We even did not have the regular electricity in my husband's place.

When my husband used to take me to my parent's house for couple of hours, my mother-in-law used to make a huge quarrel, after we returned back home. My mother-in-law was a chief in my husband's house. Nevertheless, I never showed my attitude to my husband's relatives. I never talked back to the parents of my husband and his sisters.

But my husband's parents and sisters were very rude to me. I had a tough time, living with them. I dreamed to live in a separate place with my husband and our two children. I wanted to live without my husband's relatives.

I gave birth to my first child – to my son. My husband started dating the other women. I caught him several times. I left him and I went to live with my parents. A few days later, I found out that I was pregnant with my second child. I did not want to make an abortion. My parents told me that they would take care of my children and me.

After a month, my husband bought three-bedroom apartment for our family. He came to my parent's house and told me that he was sorry for his actions. He asked me to live with him. I decided to forgive him, because I loved him. I forgave my husband and we started to live in our apartment without his relatives.

While we were living in a separate apartment with my husband, his relatives became very mad at me. They started to tell more bad things about me. My husband's relatives wanted him to divorce with me and marry another girl, who could take care of their bulls. At that time, I gave birth to my second child - my daughter.

During the daytime my husband used to be with his relatives

in the village and he used to come back to our apartment very late everyday. When he used to come home, he was very angry and mad at me. He used to tell me everything that his relatives told about me. His relatives asked him to make me live with them in the village and do all the works about their house. He told me to clean, wash and cook for them.

We used to fight a lot for that reason. As a result, I had to go back to the village and live there, with my husband's parents, his sisters and their kids. There were a lot of people in their house. It seemed to me that my husband's relatives became nice to me. They were talking nice with me, but they used to tell him that I had been bad and lazy all the time. I did not know about that. They used to tell him all those things, when I was not there (behind my back).

One day, my husband came and told me that he could not live in such a stressful life any longer. I was very surprised, because we were living together with his relatives, as he wanted and everything was all right between us. I used to do all the work about the house. So, I asked my husband to explain the reason that pushed him to make such a serious decision. He explained that his parents were telling him every day, that I had been a very bad wife for him and they did not want him to live with me. My husband said he did not need any wife next to him. He said he would drop me back to my parent's house and he would divorce with me. I agreed with him.

My husband took our two children and me, and dropped us to my parent's house. My son was three and a half years old. My daughter was two years and six months at that time. He dropped me to my parent's house and left our two children and me alone there, without a food and money.

My parents were in the USA that time, since they had the US Green Card. My parents used to live in America most of the time and they used to visit me once a year in our native country. They used to spend one month in a year in our native country. The rest of the time my parents had been living in the USA.

I was sitting in my parent's house with my two little children alone. There was a huge house, my two children and I. That was so sad and scary to me. I put my children to sleep. Then, I went to my father's room and I closed the door of that room. Then, I started to weep, sitting alone in that small room. I spoke with the Most High God a lot. I said to my Heavenly Father: "My Dear Father, as you see, nobody needs me and my two children. My husband left me with our two young children in that huge house. I am very scared. I am alone. Why? Why this had happened to me? I did not do anything wrong to him or his relatives. I was doing all the works about their house. I was cooking, washing, cleaning for them and I was taking care of my two young children as well. Why people are being rude, unfair and mean to me from my childhood? How shall we live without my husband? How shall I take care of two children without my husband's help?" I wept and wept a lot. I spent almost five hours, crying in that small room. I thought I would have a heart attack that day from the stress, I had.

Suddenly, I remembered that I had to take care of my two innocent, little kids. I remembered that I needed to live for my children. I remembered that I was responsible for the lives of my two children. I remembered the place, where my father left money just in case of emergency. I took that money.

From the early morning, we went to the store with my children and we bought all the necessary food for us. I cooked the food for us and I tried to forget about the problems of my life. I turned on the TV and I started to change the channels of the TV. Suddenly, I found a channel CNL (http://cnl.info/cnl's-mission-statement) - the channel, where a pastor was speaking about the Bible and God's words.

The pastor said: "May be you are alone right now. May be your loved one left you. God is talking to you right now, telling you that you are not alone. God is your Provider. God is your Spouse. God is your Vindicator. God will supply all your needs. God will protect you from your enemies. Rely only on God."

As soon as I had heard those words, I stopped checking other channels and I started to listen to this Pastor. I started to cry again, but that time from the happiness, because I had received the answers for the situation that I had at that period of my life. Couple of hours ago, I had asked the Most High God to help me to provide my children and myself with the food and everything we needed, since I did not have a job. I was crying that Almighty God had heard me and answered me so fast. I was so impressed how Almighty God was giving me the answers, with the help of the CNL channel (http://cnl.info/cnl's-mission-statement) and pastors.

From that day on, I started to listen to that channel day and night. I even fell asleep by listening to this channel.

Little by little, I learnt many things about Jesus Christ. Then, I found another channel TBN (http://tbn-tv.ru). It was also the channel, where the pastors used to speak about Almighty God and the Bible.

One day, for the first time in my life, I listened and watched the video of *"God's Love Letter"* on TBN channel. This *"God's Love Letter"* had changed my point of view about Almighty God. I used to think that God was angry with me and I thought that was the main reason, why I always had the problems in my life. I thought the Most High God was punishing me, by giving me the difficult and unhappy life, and by taking away from me those people that I loved (my husband, my relatives were in the USA). Here is that Letter from Our God (Our Heavenly Father) from the TBN TV (http://tbn-tv.ru) channel that had changed my entire life (You can also find this video-letter on You Tube link *"God's love letter for you"* https://youtu.be/VRMUapYeqMw):

### *"God's Love Letter for you"*

*The words you are about to experience*

**Are true**

*They will change your life*

**If you let them**

*For they come from the very Heart of God*

**He loves you**

*And He is the Father*

**You have been looking for all your life**

*This is His Love Letter to you:*

*My Child, You may not know me but I know*

*everything about you. (Psalm 139:1)*

*I know when you sit down and when you rise up. (Psalm 139:2)*

*I am familiar with all your ways (Psalm 139:3)*

*Even the very hairs on your head are*

*numbered. (Matthew 10:29-31)*

*For you were made in my image (Genesis 1:27)*

*In Me you live and move and have your being. (Acts 17:28)*

*For you are my offspring. (Acts 17:28)*

*I knew you even before you were conceived. (Jeremiah 1:4-5)*

*I chose you when I planned creation (Ephesians 1:11-12)*

*You were not a mistake. (Psalm 139:15-16)*

*For all your days are written in my Book. (Psalm 139:15-16)*

*I determined the exact time of your birth and*

*where you would live. (Acts 17:26)*

*You are fearfully and wonderfully made. (Psalm 139:14)*

*I knit you together in your mother's womb. (Psalm 139:13)*

*And brought you forth on the day you were born. (Psalm 71:6)*

*I have been misrepresented by those who*

*don't know me. (John 8:41-44)*

*I am not distant and angry, but I am the*

*complete expression of love. (I John 4:16)*

*And it is my desire to lavish my love on you (I John 3:1)*

*Simply because you are my child and I*

*am your Father. (I John 3:1)*

*I offer you more than your earthly father*

*ever could. (Matthew 7:11)*

*For I am the perfect Father. (Matthew 5:48)*

*Every good gift that you receive comes*

*from My Hand. (James 1:17)*

*For I am your Provider and I meet all*

*your needs. (Matthew 6:31-33)*

*My Plans for your future has always been*

*filled with hope. (Jeremiah 29:11)*

*Because I love you with an everlasting love. (Jeremiah 31:3)*

*My thoughts toward you are countless as the*

*sand on the seashore. (Psalm 139:17-18)*

*And I rejoice over you with singing. (Zephaniah 3:17)*

*I will never stop doing good to you. (Jeremiah 32:40)*

*For you are my treasured possession. (Exodus 19:5)*

*I desire to establish you with all My Heart*

*and all My Soul. (Jeremiah 32:41)*

*And I want to show you great and*
*marvelous things. (Jeremiah 33:3)*
*If you seek me with all your heart, you*
*will find me. (Deuteronomy 4:29)*
*Delight in me and I will give you the*
*desires of your heart. (Psalm 37:4)*
*For it is I who gave you those desires. (Philippians 2:13)*
*I am able to do more for you than you could*
*possibly imagine. (Ephesians 3:20)*
*For I am your greatest encourager. (2 Thessalonians 2:16-17)*
*I am also the Father who comforts you in all*
*your troubles. (2 Corinthians 1:3-4)*
*When you are brokenhearted, I am close to you. (Psalm 34:18)*
*As a shepherd carries a lamb, I have carried*
*you close to my heart. (Isaiah 40:11)*
*One day I will wipe away every tear from*
*your eyes. (Revelation 21:3-4)*
*And I will take away all the pain you have*
*suffered on this Earth. (Revelation 21:3-4)*
*I am your Father and I love you even as I*
*love my son, Jesus. (John 17:23)*
*For in Jesus, My Love for you is revealed. (John 17:26)*
*He is the exact representation of My Being. (Hebrews 1:3)*
*He came to demonstrate that I am for you,*
*not against you. (Romans 8:31)*

*And to tell you that I am not counting*
*your sins. (2 Corinthians 5:18-19)*
*Jesus died so that you and I could be*
*reconciled. (2 Corinthians 5:18-19)*
*His death was the ultimate expression of*
*My Love for you. (1 John 4:10)*
*I gave up everything I loved that I might*
*gain your love. (Romans 8:32)*
*If you receive the gift of My Son Jesus,*
*you receive me. (1 John 2:23)*
*And nothing will ever separate you from*
*My Love again. (Romans 8:38-39)*
*Come home and I'll throw the Biggest Party*
*Heaven has ever seen. (Luke 15:7)*
*I have always been Father and will always*
*be Father. (Ephesians 3:14-15)*
***My Question is … Will you be My Child?*** *(John 1:12-13)*
*I am waiting for you. (Luke 15:11-32)*
***Love, Your Dad***
***Almighty God.***

This video-letter from the Most High God was taken from the Bible and it had changed my attitude to my entire life. I understood that there was a hope for my two children and me. One day, I learnt from the CNL channel (http://cnl.info/cnl's-mission-statement) that Almighty God wants us to believe in a better life, but never trust the bad events, in which we are living at a certain period of our lives. I understood that even though we had some problems and loneliness in our lives, we should never think that those problems would stay with us for the rest of our lives. God will never allow unhappiness; bad break to take deep roots in our lives. I had heard from the Pastor from CNL channel (http://cnl.info/cnl's-mission-statement) that we should not believe in what our eyes were seeing, but we had to rely, trust and believe in our dreams, and in the things, which our heart was telling us. We have to believe in the fact that we will have a better life in the future. We need to remind ourselves that the best days of our lives are ahead of us. I mean we need to know that those bad events took place in order to bring the happiness into our lives and they will be with us temporary, but not permanently.

The Most High God allows negative things to happen to us, if only God has a perfect plan to use those negative events to raise us higher, improve our lives, move us into the higher level and bring the huge positive changes into our lives.

The thing is during those days, when I was alone with my two children without help; I did not have this knowledge about Almighty God. I was not aware that God would use the obstacles and problems to bring the happiness in our lives. I did not know those obstacles and problems were meant to make us stronger. My parents and relatives did not teach me this truth about Almighty God and about how God plans everything in our lives for the better. I used to listen to "God's Love Letter" every night before sleeping several times. While I was listening to God's promises through this video-letter, I used to weep from the happiness that I was not alone in the middle of that difficult situation.

I started to look for a job at that time. My aunt had a huge Pharmacy and I asked her, if she could give me a job to earn my livings. I enrolled my two children into the Day Care center that was close to my parent's house, where we used to live. I started to work in the pharmacy. I had a hope inside of my heart that one day the Most High God would make us happy (my two children and me). My parents started to support us, by sending us some money for paying our bills and other expenses. I started to pay attention to myself, by dressing up the pretty clothes. Whenever I had a free time, I used to listen to the CNL channel (http://cnl.info/cnl's-mission-statement) to learn more about the Bible and God's words. I believe, this knowledge gave me the strength to continue my life, fighting for our happiness during those difficult times, trusting and relying on Almighty God.

One Day, I was at my work in that Pharmacy and my father-in-law came to the Pharmacy with my mother-in-law to speak with my aunt. They spoke with my aunt about me, telling her that I was a very bad wife for their son. I heard every word they told my aunt about my parents and me. Suddenly, my aunt stopped my father-in-law and told him that if I had been such a bad wife and bad daughter-in-law, then why they came to take me back to their place to live with their son. To tell you the truth, I was so glad to hear that somebody was protecting me.

Then, my father-in-law answered that they did not want their grandchildren (my two kids) to live without father. My aunt told them, I needed some time to think about returning back to their family. The same day, after our work my aunt gave me a very wise advice – she told me that I had two ways out from that situation.

The first way out: I should go back to my husband and his parents, cause they came to my work to take me back to their family. In that case I had to accept my husband and all his relatives, with all their negative features, and live with them.

The second way out: I should not trust them anymore and I should work, and support my kids; and try to build my future without my husband and his family. In that case, some day I would meet someone to be with and someone, who would make me happy.

I made a decision to choose the first way out – to return back to my husband and live with him, and with all his relatives, taking care of them. I made that choice, because I did not want my neighbors to gossip about me at that time.

People would think negative things about woman, who had

divorced in my native country. People used to make a lot of gossip in such kind of situation.

Next day, my father-in-law came to the Pharmacy to take my kids and me back to their place, together with my mother-in-law. I took my two children from the day care and we went back to the village with the parents of my husband. I was waiting for my husband to come home from his meat store to talk with him. He came very late at that night. When he saw me, my husband became very angry. He started to fight with his parents, telling them that he did not love me and he did not want to live with me anymore. I was very surprised to hear that, because I thought my husband had asked his parents to bring our two kids and me back home to live with him.

My husband screamed at his parents, telling them he would not live together with our children and me. Then, he left. He did not come home for two more days. Then, he started to come during the daytime to check his bulls and he used to leave. I was crying every night, while waiting for my husband to come back home. I did not leave my husband's home and his parents, because my mother-in-law came to my room and she asked me to stay with them, and to give my husband more time to make up his mind. My mother-in-law mentioned that I had to forgive him, since other men could also make such kind of mistake and betray their wives. She also informed me that her son was living in his sister's house in order not to live with us.

It is very hard for me to write about those days from my life, because I am reminding myself about those painful nights, which I spent crying and waiting for my ex-husband to come back home. But, the only thing that helped me to survive during those days was "God's Love Letter", which I mentioned earlier. I used to weep and watch that video-letter from the Most High God every day before sleeping many times, again and again.

My mother-in-law changed her attitude towards me. We became friends with her. She told me that she used to follow the advices of her older daughter during those days, when she used to tell the negative things about me. She informed me that her older daughter used to tell her to be rude with me in order to be able to control me. She mentioned she was very sorry that she used to listen to her older daughter's advises, since my mother-in-law could not control my husband anymore without my help. My mother-in-law understood that her son had another woman and the woman was controlling him. That was the reason why my husband did not listen to his parents anymore.

After several weeks, we started to live with my husband together. My husband came back home, but he informed me that he had met another woman, and she was willing to live with him.

One day, I asked Almighty God to help me to make the right choice in my life, because I knew that my husband had another woman. I asked Almighty God if I should forgive my husband

and his relatives, and live with them or if I should leave my husband and divorce with him. After coupe of days, I received the answer, while listening to the CNL TV channel (http://cnl. info/cnl's-mission-statement), where the preacher spoke about the forgiveness.

My parents advised me to divorce with my husband. They told me not to forgive my husband and his relatives. I remembered, one day my mother called me from the USA and told me not to live with my husband. She told me not to do any work about their house. My mother even screamed at me through the phone. I explained my mother that I should forgive my enemies and pray for them. Only then, Almighty God would bless me for the unfair situations, which I had in my life. Only then, the Most High God would punish my enemies in its time. I told my mother that I would choose to listen to God's advice, which was to forgive my enemies and pray for them.

I forgave him. I continued to live with my husband and his relatives. I was relying on God's words that we need to forgive our enemies, and we had to do the good things to our enemies. I used to listen to the CNL channel, where the Pastors used to preach about the forgiveness and power to forgive our enemies. I relied on God's words that we need to do the positive things to our enemies and pray for them. Only then, God would reward us. Almighty God told everybody could do the good things to their friends, but not everybody had the power to forgive their enemies and do the good things to them. God also mentioned in the Bible that we were supposed to be like the Most High God. Since, God gives the sun, rain, and snow to the "good" people and "sinners" as well. We also believe that we belong to Almighty God. Then, we are supposed to act like Our Heavenly Father.

My husband left to another country to earn some money. He dropped our kids and me to my parent's house.

Before those events, approximately one year ago, my husband had infected me with a genitally transmitted disease –trichomoniasis. When my gynecologist informed me about it, I was shocked. Of course, this news was very painful for me to live with. I decided to have a revenge on my husband, by finding any other man and spending with him a night. The same day, I saw the Vision that scared me a lot. In that Dream I heard a very strong voice (a man's voice). That voice told me: "I am the Creator of everything in this World. I am controlling everything, everywhere and forever. Only I have the right to revenge on somebody. You don't have a right to revenge. I am aware of everything that is happening to you and I know the person, who is guilty for your unhappiness. Look at that person! She is responsible for your problems. Look how I will punish that person!" I looked at the woman and I recognized my mother-in-law. She was walking and, suddenly, the fire came to her from the sky. My mother-in-law was burning and screaming. I got really scared. In 2 minutes my mother-in-law turned into the dark dust.

The voice told me: "Did you see what I have done to her? I will punish anybody, who tries to hurt you or did hurt you. But you do not have the right to revenge. Do not try to get a revenge on your enemies."

I woke up after that dream very scared. I changed my mind about having revenge on my husband. I did not know this voice was God's voice. I did not know this vision was from the Most High God either.

I realized it after one year, when my mother-in-law got gastric cancer of the third degree. We all were so upset, because she had never had any serious problems with her health until that time. I understood that only God knew the future. As it is written in the Bible: Isaiah 44:6-Isaiah 44:8 (New International Version) "This is what the LORD says - Israel's King and Redeemer, the LORD Almighty: I am the first and I am the last; apart from Me there is no God. 7. Who then I like me? Let him proclaim it. Let him declare and lay out before me what has happened since I established my ancient people, and what is yet to come—yes, let them foretell what will come. 8. Do not tremble, do not be afraid. Did I not proclaim this and foretell it long ago? You are my witnesses. Is there any God besides me? No, there is no other Rock; I know not one."

We informed my husband to come back to our country,

because his mother had the gastric cancer of the third degree. He returned back as soon as he had the chance. I took my mother-in-law to an oncologist, where she could have chemotherapy. She had to have the surgery on her stomach and then, the chemotherapy. But my father-in-law refused to allow her to have this surgery and chemotherapy.

Instead of that, my father-in-law took her to the folk healers. Of course, the folk healers did not help my mother-in-law. I used to live with my husband and his parents at that time. I left my job and I used to take care of my mother-in-law.

My mother-in-law asked an apology from me, for the negative things she had done to me, and for the lies, she used to tell about me to other people. She said that I had been better than her daughters, since her daughters did not take care of her, when she got the cancer. I was sitting next to her most of the time, while her daughters and my husband used to work.

One day my aunts came to visit my mother-in-law. My mother-in-law told them that she was so happy to have such daughter-in-law like me. She also told my relatives that I used to take care of her better than her daughters. My relatives were really surprised, because couple of years ago my mother-in-law used to tell them that I had been a very lazy and bad daughter-in-law.

My mother-in-law's health condition was getting worse and worse every day, because she refused to have the chemotherapy.

She started to have a strong pain all over her body. Doctors explained me that the pain she had, used to come from the cells of her body, which were dying due to the cancer. She felt the strong pain on herself, when every cell of her body was dying. I realized this pain was the same like in the situation, when a person got burned. Then I remembered my Dream, when the Most High God showed me how my mother-in-law had been walking and, suddenly, the fire came from the sky, and she was on the fire, and she got burned. The dark dust on the ground was left from her. I understood that Almighty God showed me beforehand how He would take the revenge on my enemies. Only after one year, I understood the meaning of that Vision and I found out that the strong man's voice was the Most High God's voice, since only God knew (and knows) our future.

I used to sit next to my mother-in-law most of the time. During the last minutes of her breath, I fell asleep and I saw another dream, with the same voice that was really scary to me. Unfortunately, I do not remember every word that I was told, but I remember the main idea. The voice told me: "Never give up. I am your Creator and the Creator of the Universe. I created everything. I will support you. I will supply all your needs. Rely only on me. Look only ahead. Live thinking about your happy future. Forget your past. Go to the Future all the time. Never give up. When people will make the evil to you, never give up. My hand will be next to you, protecting you. I will take all the bad things that people might do against you and I will change them into good for you, and I will return them as the good things to you. Go to your Dreams. Live for your Dreams. Do not forget about your Dreams. Remember your Dreams. Read My Book day and night. My Book should be in your hands day and night. And My Words should come out of your mouth day and night. I will put the Angels next to you and they will protect you in every step you take. My angels will protect you day and night. Your Name is written in My "Book of Life". Your days are written in My "Book of Life". Look at this Book."

Then, I saw a Huge Book standing on the air. That Book was like a huge computer, but with two screens, where I could see my life. I saw my life and my Dreams. The voice told me: "I know all your Dreams. Go for your Dreams. Go forwards and reach your Dreams. I will help you to reach your Dreams."

Then, I saw the second Book that was standing on the air. That Book was on the fire, but the Book did not get burned. This Book had words and sentences. I was really surprised on how the Book, being on the fire, was still safe and could not get burned. The Book was open and the Most High God spoke the words that I could follow and read from the second Book, which was on the fire and on the air. The Most High God told me that I could find all His promises in His Book – in the BIBLE. The second Book was the BIBLE.

I believe that all those promises, which Almighty God told me, belong to EVERY SINGLE CHILD of the Most High God.

When I just opened my eyes I saw how my mother-in-law had her last breath and she passed away.

I got some questions inside of my heart that made me worried and think about. Why God told me if people make me the evil or bad things, Almighty God would change them for good to me, and I should not give up or worry. I had very positive relationship with my husband at that time. His relatives were also nice to me. Then, why did the Most High God tell me that people might hurt me? Who could hurt me? Why?

I needed almost one year to find the answers to those questions. After my mother-in-law's death, we moved to my parent's house with my husband and my kids, because my sister-in-law moved to our village house to live with my father-in-law. It was my husband's decision to move to my parent's house, as his sister used to steal my dresses, shoes and even my underwear.

My husband used to work at daytime and he used to come home after his job every day. Everything was good. We did not have any more quarrels with my husband. But inside of my heart I felt that something was wrong.

My father came from the USA and told me that one of the huge companies wanted to write a book and booklet about their products, and the company itself. My father said if that company liked my book and booklet, they would offer me a job of a manager at their company. So, I decided to try my success. I wrote the book and booklet, and I handled them to the company. Then, I waited for their decision. Later, I received a phone call from them inviting me for a job. I accepted that offer and I started to work as a manager at the company.

Meanwhile, I went to the church in my native country and I bought the Bible, since Almighty God told me to have His book in my hand - the BIBLE - always and talk about God's words all the time. I started reading the Bible. I really learned a lot of useful and important things about our lives. I found the answers to all the questions about my life. I also found the answers to the questions that I had asked Almighty God.

I found the explanations to almost all my Dreams. First of all, I found God's words that I had heard in my Dreams in the Bible (New International Version): "Psalm 91.1- 16.

1.  Whoever dwells in the shelter of the Most High will rest in the shadow of the Almighty.
2.  I will say of the LORD, "He is my refuge and my fortress, my God in whom I trust."
3.  Surely He will save you from the fowler's snare and from the deadly pestilence.
4.  He will cover you with His feathers, and under His wings you will find refuge; His faithfulness will be your shield and rampart.

5.   You will not fear the terror of night, nor the arrow that flies by day,

6.   nor the pestilence that stalks in the darkness, nor the plague that destroys at midday.

7.   A thousand may fall at your side, ten thousand at your right hand, but it will not come near you.

8.   You will only observe with your eyes and see the punishment of the wicked.

9.   If you say, "The LORD is my refuge," and you make the Most High your dwelling,

10. no harm will overtake you, no disaster will come near your tent.

11. For He will command His angels concerning you to guard you in all your ways;

12. They will lift you up on their hands, so that you will not strike your foot against a stone;

13. You will tread on the lion and the cobra; you will trample the great lion and the serpent.

14. "Because he loves me," says the LORD, "I will rescue him; I will protect him, for he acknowledges my name.

15. He will call on me, and I will answer him; I will be with him in trouble, I will deliver him and honor him.

16. With long life I will satisfy him and show him my salvation."

Isaiah 59:20 (Bible, New International Version) .The Redeemer will come to Zion, to those in Jacob who repent of their sins", declares the LORD.

Isaiah 59:21. (Bible, New Living Translation) " And this is my covenant with them", says the LORD. "My spirit will not leave them, and neither will these words I have given you. They will be on your lips and on the lips of your children and your children's children forever. I, the LORD, have spoken!

Then, I saw another Vision, where I was hanging down from the mountain, trying to save my life. I saw a man with white cloth on, with a camel walking on the same straight mountain. I was very surprised on how a person could walk so easily on such a high and straight mountain, when I was hanging down from the same mountain, trying to hold on a rock in order not to fall down. Then, I called that man - Adam. I said to Him: "Adam, Adam! Don't you see I am almost falling down from this mountain? You have to help me! Help me please!" The man looked down at me and told me that if he helped me than I would have to change my life, and I would have to live following all His rules during my life. I agreed with the man. He helped me and he told me that he would change my entire life.

During several months, I tried to find out who was that man, called Adam. How did I know his name in my vision? The first man's name, created by Almighty God, had been Adam. I was aware of that, but I was sure Adam, who saved me and prevented me from falling down the mountain, had more Power and Glory. I was sure the person, who saved me, was not the first Adam, created by the Most High God.

In the Bible I found the following information:

> 1 Corinthians 15:45 (New Living Translation) The Scripture tell us, "The first man, Adam, became a living person." But the last Adam –that is, Christ—is a life-giving Spirit. So I found out that Adam that saved me was Jesus Christ. With the help of my last dream, God showed me that I was supposed to be baptized.

I spoke with the Pastor of the church and I told him about the Dreams I had. The Pastor told me to be very careful with our Dreams, because some of our Dreams could be from God and some of them could be from Evil. I decided for myself that time would show me the real meaning of my visions.

I told the Pastor I needed to be baptized. Pastor said I needed to think about that decision, cause I came from the Muslim family. My parents and all my relatives were against my decision. My husband did not care about that. So, I made up my mind and I was baptized at that church. I did not baptize my two children, because I wanted my kids to make their own choice in that area of their life.

My children had been baptized in the USA, when we moved

there. I used to visit a church several times a month in America. Once the Pastor came to me, when I was sitting and praying at that church, and he asked me, if I baptized my two children, because I used to take my children with me to the church. I told the pastor that I decided to wait until my children would make their own choice to be baptized or not. The pastor told me that I was wrong and I should have done that at the same time, when I was baptized. The pastor told me I made the right choice, when I decided to accept Jesus Christ into my life as my Redeemer, but I did not think about my children's life and about saving their souls. I felt so selfish after his words. Then, I spoke with my children about Jesus Christ and I asked them, if they wanted to be baptized and accept the LORD as their Savior. My children agreed with me and we went to the church. The Pastor baptized my two children, when they were 10 and 11 years old.

I realized that God sent the Pastor of that church, to give me the message from Almighty God that changed my children's entire life for the best. I was so thankful to the Most High God for His help.

At the present time, my two children are teenagers and they do read the Bible every day and they have a good knowledge about God.

Now, I want to go back to my past and talk about the period of my life, when I still had been in my native country.

I started to pray differently after reading the Bible. I started looking differently at my life. My heart became full of the happiness and satisfaction after reading the Bible. The Bible changed my life. The feeling of the stress disappeared from my heart. I started to understand that not everything depended on us. I understood that everything in our lives used to happen for a reason. Almighty God allowed some negative things to happen in our lives for a reason. The Most High God used our mistakes, obstacles, and problems to bring us higher for the better level.

I was still working as a manager at the company and I started to see the same vision every day. I saw how my elder sister-in-law was cooking the breads and food, and she used to bring those foods to the family of a young woman, who was going to marry my husband. I saw in my dream how my father-in-law used to visit the parents of the young woman, asking them to let her marry my husband. I did not pay a great attention to those dreams.

One day, my husband left his phone at home. I took his phone and I looked at his messages, because I used to see those dreams every day. I never checked his cell phone before, as my husband never allowed me to look at his messages and his cell phone. I saw the messages sent by my husband to a young woman, telling her that he loved her so much, and he could not live without her. My husband did not even erase those messages from his cell phone.

Next day, I went to my work and I called that young woman.

I asked her what kind of relationships she had with my husband. She said she wanted to see me. I asked her to come to my work and I gave her the address, where I used to work. She came to my work and she informed me that my husband's elder sister, together with my father-in-law, used to go to her parents with lots of homemade foods, asking her to marry my husband. My father-in-law and his daughter told them, as if I took our two children and run away with a man to the USA, because my parents had been living in America for several years already. The young woman and her family believed in everything that my husband (together with his father and sister) told them about me. I understood that all my dreams were true. My dreams were informing me that my husband was trying to marry another woman, being married with me. Since a Muslim man could have several wives at one and the same time.

The woman informed me that my husband took her to a restaurant for a date. She also told me that she had a boy friend and she informed my husband about her relation with her boy friend. My husband told her, if she married him, she would forget about her boy friend. She was graduating from the medical college. She advised me to divorce with my husband, as he was such a big liar. She asked me to tell my husband to leave her alone, because her parents wanted to make her marry to my husband. They believed my husband to be a rich man, since he used to come to their house every day in the different cars, telling them that those cars belonged to him. I told her I would leave to the USA, if I had a chance, but unfortunately I did not have a visa at that time. I told her the truth that my husband used to live with our two children and me, and we had a good relationship with him. I also told her that his sisters did not like me and we had the negative relations with them. The woman advised me to divorce with my husband and she left.

I did not tell anything to my husband about the young woman, when I came back home. I pretended that nothing had happened.

After few days, my husband did not come to my parent's place, where I had been living with my two children. He did not answer his cell phone, when I called him. I went to his work to see and speak with him. He told me to go home. He promised to come home that day to explain me the reason, why he was not coming home those days. But he did not come home for several more days. I understood that something (wrong) was happening between us. I felt as if I was loosing my family. I decided to go to his parent's place, where I could find him any time. I took my two children and we went there. I did not understand myself why I went there after such terrible news. Something inside of my heart was telling me to go there and something was pushing me to go to my husband's place to save my family. I forgot about the respect to myself and I went to speak with my husband.

As soon as I came to my husband's place, I saw there many

people – my father-in-law, my sister-in-law, my husband's aunt and their grandchildren. I went to my husband's room and I decided to wait for him in his room. After two hours my elder sister-in-law came to that room and she started to fight with me. She told me that they were planning to marry my husband to another woman after one month. But the young woman told them everything that we spoke with her. The young woman and her family came to the house of my elder sister-in-law and they made a huge quarrel, telling her how they found out the truth about their huge lie. They told her that I was not in the USA and my husband used to live with me in my parent's house at that time. They brought to the shame the family of my elder sister-in-law. Then, the young woman's parents went to my husband's work and disgraced him at his work as well.

My husband came and joint his sister and they started screaming at me. They were mad at me, because I told the young woman the truth (I was still in my native country and my husband was living with me). I did not say anything back to my husband, but I told to my elder sister-in-law the following words: "I will not answer to any of your rudeness and I will not take a revenge on you for all the bad things you have been doing to me, trying to destroy my family. But I know one thing for sure, the Most High God will punish you, using your children for all the pains that you have brought into my life. You have four children and you know that it is a big sin to destroy a house of a bird, but you are trying to destroy a person's family – my family. This sin is bigger. God will punish you for me, because Almighty God is my Vindicator. I will see or hear about that in its time."

I did not know how the strength came to me to speak back to my sister-in-law. I didn't know how those meaningful words came to my heart. But I was sure that I told the right words to her that day.

My sister-in-law was leaving my husband's room and she said to my husband not to be rude with me, because the day before my husband had a terrible car crush, when he almost lost his life. My sister-in-law told my husband that Almighty God was punishing him for hurting the feelings of our two children and me. Then, she left.

That day was the worst day of my life, when I saw the real face of my husband and his sisters. I could not believe that all these events were happening to me. I was crying the whole night. I could not stop thinking of how my husband was trying to marry the second wife, lying to me. Nevertheless, I continued to live with my husband in the village with his relatives.

Later, I left my job, since my husband asked me to leave my job. He told me if I wanted to save our family, I had to leave my job of the manager. I used to live in such conditions for several months, living with my husband, who did not love me. I had been doing all the works about the house for his family, cooking for his father, sisters and their children.

My husband could not sleep with me in one room. He had to sleep in another room and I had to sleep with my children in a separate room. My husband was afraid to live with me in one room, because his father did not allow him to live with me in one room.

After several weeks, I started feeling myself very sick, vomiting all the time. I had a pain in my stomach. I was not pregnant at that time. I understood that stress was bringing some sickness to me.

At the same time, I had been reading the Bible. I came across to the place in the Bible, when the Most High God said to His people to leave the place of sin - Babylon, the place, where other people used to sin (Bible, New Living Translation):

Jeremiah 51:6 Flee from Babylon! Save yourselves! Don't get trapped in her punishment! It is the LORD's time for vengeance; He will repay her in full.

Jeremiah 51:24 "I will repay Babylon and the people of Babylonia for all the wrong they have done to my people in Jerusalem", says the LORD.

Jeremiah 51:36 This is what the LORD says to Jerusalem: "I will be your lawyer to plead your case, and I will avenge you. I will dry up her river, as well as her springs,

Jeremiah 51:37 and Babylon will become a heap of ruins, haunted by jackals. She will be an object of horror and contempt, a place where no one lives.

Jeremiah 51.45 "Come out, my people, flee from Babylon. Save yourselves! Run from the LORD's fierce anger.

Jeremiah 51:50 Get out, all you who have escaped the sword! Do not stand and watch—flee while you can! Remember the LORD, though you are in a far-off land, and think about your home in Jerusalem."

I understood that those words were concerning my life and me. I understood that I had to leave their house, where my father-in-law had been living with his daughters and their children. They were earning money by doing dark magic to other people and by telling people their future like the fortune-tellers. They were lying to the people, who trusted them. I understood that place, where I had been living with my children, was like Babylon in front of God's Eyes. As a parent, we do not want our children to be friends with the negative people. I understood that Almighty God did not want me to live with such kind of people like my husband and his relatives.

I also understood, while reading the Bible that until I had been with my husband and his relatives, the Most High God could not punish them. Since God could hurt my children and me. I realized that I was interrupting the Most High God to complete His plan and I had been disobeying My Heavenly Father for a long time.

My father-in-law used to earn a lot of money by doing the dark magic to the people for many years. A lot of people knew that my father-in-law used to make the dark magic for an expensive fee. He used to spend most of his earnings to buy the drugs for himself. Every year my father-in-law used to pilgrimage to Mecca city of Saudi Arabiya. He used to wear the white, long cloths like the prophets used to do. People used to think that my father-in-law had been so pure and holy man. My parents agreed to marry me to his son for that reason. We were sure that every person, who used to pilgrimage to such Holy place like Mecca, would be a generous, kind and sincere person. I could not understand how a person would bring a lot of pain to other people in order to earn some money. At the same time that person had been pretending to be very pure, kind and holy person.

My father-in-law always used to hurt my feelings. He used to sit next to my husband and me for two hours, talking the negative things about my parents and me. He used to tell that I would never be a nice wife and my parents were so bad people, and on and on. I used to sit and listen to such kind of words, without the right to say a word to protect my parents or me. I used to do all the works about the house for them and, as a result, I had to listen to many negative words, and thoughts from my father-in-law, and my husband towards my parents and me.

After reading the part from the Bible, where Almighty God told His people to leave the Babylon, I felt that I had to leave those people. (Bible, New International Version) Isaiah 48: 20

Leave Babylon, flee from the Babylonians! Announce this with shouts of joy and proclaim it. Send it out to the ends of the earth; say, "The LORD has redeemed his servant Jacob."

I understood that if I decided to stay there, I would be punished too by Almighty God. My life there was getting worse and worse. Since, I was living in my husband's house with his relatives like a slave without the right to talk or say anything. I decided to leave such life. I decided to let my husband go and live without us. I was tired of fighting for my husband's love and I decided to give up. Unfortunately, I even used to go to some fortune-tellers to win my husband's love back. At that time, I did not know that it was a huge sin against Almighty God. When I pray today, I am still asking the Most High God to forgive me for visiting the fortune-tellers.

I did pack up my cloths and I informed my husband that I would leave him alone, so he could marry anybody he wanted. My husband did not even try to stop me, as he had another woman on the side. I knew he had a woman dating at his work.

When I was leaving with my son and daughter, my father-in-law stopped me and said that he would make his dark magic against me, and he would kill me with his dark magic, if I decided to leave his son. I answered to my father-in-law that the Most High God gave my life and the chance to live, and only Almighty God could take my life, but nobody else except Almighty God. That was my answer to my father-in-law. I left his place with my children to live in my parent's house. I relied on God's words. That is why I left my husband and his relatives. I did not want my children to be like them and to make the dark magic to people. I did not want the Most High God to punish my children for their grandfather's sins.

When I came to my parent's home, I was alone with my children again, since my parents were in America at that time. I went to my father's small room and I started to weep. I spoke to the Most High God very sincerely. I said to Almighty God that I left my past and my past mistakes, and sins, relying on God and on His words. I asked the Most High God to forgive me, for I had visited the fortune-tellers many times. I asked Almighty God's help and Forgiveness. I asked the Most High God to give me the real Love that I had never had in my life, as I had to marry with my husband, without being in love with him. My husband never loved me. I asked Almighty God to give me the husband from Him – the husband from the Most High God. I asked God to give me such husband, who would love me the way I was and who would appreciate everything I would do for him: my works, my efforts to improve our lives, my love and loyalty to him.

I also asked the Most High God to make my husband to be very sorry for he did not appreciate his wife (me), son and daughter. I really asked God to show my husband that he had been wrong with me, by being rude with me, and having another women dating most of the time, and not paying attention to his son and daughter. I asked God of Israel to be my Vindicator during my entire life.

As for me, I forgave my husband and all his relatives, who did hurt my feelings and took an active part in ruining my life, and my family.

In two weeks, I went back to my work of a manager. My parents came back from America for two months in summer. My parents had to finish their construction work in their house, because they were building a new house in their yard.

I had my own three-bedroom apartment, where I could live with my children at that time. If I decided to live in my own apartment, everybody in our country would think the negative things about me. The people would think that I became a bad woman, dating different men in my own apartment. I did not want people to gossip about me and my life. I had to live in my parent's house in order not to be involved in people's gossip.

One day, I went into my apartment to bring some clothes from there. I found some things there that belonged to another woman. I understood that my husband had a date with a woman in my apartment. He left those things for me to know about his girlfriends. In this way he wanted to hurt my feelings. I called him and I asked him not to bring his girlfriends into my apartment, cause he had his own apartments. I informed my husband that I would repair my apartment and later, I would live with our two children in there. My husband said to me ironically to repair "very poor and old house"(as he said) of my parents first of all, where I had been living, and then I should repair my apartment. Those words hurt me very much. At that time my parent's house was really old and it needed to be repaired, but my parents did not have enough money to do so. They spent almost three years to earn some money to build a new house in their place. While I was reading the Bible, I found God's Words telling that God of Israel would destroy the old house and build a new one. I felt like these words were concerning my life (Bible, New Living Translation):

Isaiah 58:11 The LORD will guide you continually, giving you water when you are dry and restoring your strength. You will be like a well-watered garden, like an ever-flowing spring.

Isaiah 58:12 Some of you will rebuild the deserted ruins of your cities. Then you will be known as a rebuilder of walls and a restorer of homes.

I understood that Almighty God was telling me through the Bible, that God would destroy old house of my parents and build a new house for us. While reading the following passage from the Bible, I had heard the voice telling me that Almighty God would Bless us, and nobody would call us abandoned, but people would call us Blessed. I also accepted these words from the Most High God, believing that later on, the Most High God would help my children and me (Bible, New Living Translation):

Isaiah 62:1. Because I love Zion, I will not keep still. Because my heart yearns for Jerusalem, I cannot remain silent. I will not stop praying for her until her righteousness shines like the dawn, and her salvation blazes like a burning torch.

Isaiah 62:2. The nations will see your righteousness. World leaders will be blinded by your glory. And you will be given a new name by the LORD'S Own Mouth.

Isaiah 62:3. The LORD will hold you in His Hand for all to see – a splendid crown in the hand of God.

Isaiah 62:4. Never again you will be called "The Forsaken City" or "The Desolate Land". Your new name will be "The City of God's Delight" and "The Bride of God", for the LORD delights in you and will claim you as his bride.

Isaiah 62:5. Your children will commit themselves to you, O Jerusalem, just as a young man commits himself to his bride. Then God will rejoice over you as a bridegroom rejoices over his bride.

Isaiah 62:6. O Jerusalem, I have posted watchmen on your walls; they will pray day and night, continually. Take no rest, all you who pray to the LORD.

Isaiah 62:7. Give the LORD no rest until he completes his work, until He makes Jerusalem the pride of the earth.

Isaiah 62:8. The LORD has sworn to Jerusalem by His own strength: "I will never again hand you over to your enemies.

Never again will foreign warriors come and take away your grain and new wine.

Isaiah 62:9. You raised the grain, and you will eat it, praising the LORD. Within the courtyards of the Temple, you yourselves will drink the wine you have pressed".

Isaiah 62:10. Go out through the gates! Prepare the highway for my people to return! Smooth out the road; pull out the boulders; raise a flag for all the nations to see.

Isaiah 62:11. The LORD has sent this message to every land: "Tell the people of Israel, Look, your Savior is coming. See, He brings His reward with Him as He comes."

Isaiah 62:12. They will be called "The Holy People" and "The People Redeemed by the LORD." And Jerusalem will be known as "The Desirable Place" and "The City No Longer Forsaken."

I went to a lawyer and I started our divorcing process. I was living with my parents in their house. My parents were helping me a lot, supplying my children and me with the food, shelter and advices. I used to go to my work. Then, I used to spent time with my children. My parents started to build their new house. There were many people, who used to come everyday to build their new house.

Almost six months passed and I had been living in the same way. Nothing had changed in my life. I went to the court, where I was called to speak with the judge about my divorce process. I went there with my lawyer and we met my husband with his lawyer. The judge called me and asked me why I decided to divorce with him, since we had had two children. I explained the judge that my husband wanted to marry another woman, being married with me and he used to date with other women. The judge told me that my husband had the right to have as many wives as he could feed, and my job was to be with him and obey him all the time. I was really shocked by those words of the judge. I thought that I would find the justice in the court, but I found the same betrayal. So, I just asked the judge to divorce us, because I would not change my mind.

I lived with my parents for couple of weeks more, reading the Bible and talking about Jesus Christ to my parents and my relatives. My sister had been living in the USA and my brother was in Moscow at that time. I used to write them on email about Jesus Christ. Nobody from my relatives agreed with my decision to read the Bible. But I used to read the Bible and I used to watch the channels, where the Pastors preached God's words and Gospel.

One day another miracle happened to me. That was the day, when my life started to change for good. That was the day, when my dreams came true. I was sitting at my work, when my father called me and he was so excited. My father asked me to give him my passport. I asked him the reason why he needed it. He told me that I won the Green Card lottery game. He informed me that I could become the permanent resident of the USA together with my two children. I asked my father not to make such kind of jokes with me, because I had been dreaming about that for almost 10 years.

My father told me that he was telling me the truth about winning the lottery game of Green Card. I asked a permission to leave my work earlier that day and I went home. When I came home, my mother was almost crying from the happiness that my dream to move to the USA came true at last. She was so happy for me.

I started to weep from my happiness that Almighty God had heard my praying and gave me even more, than I had asked Him. I still had a doubt that somebody else had won instead of me, someone with the same first and last name like mine. After two weeks, I received my package from the post office, proving that I really won the Green Card lottery game together with my two children. I had been participating at the Green Card lottery Game during seven years. After seven years of participating, Almighty God gave me the chance to live, work and study in the USA.

Now, I had one big problem – I had to get a written permission from my ex-husband to our children to leave our native country. We thought with my parents about the way out from that situation. Then, my father went to my ex-husband to speak with him about the Green Card and about moving to the USA. My father asked him to give me the written permission to our children to leave our native country, because without his permission our children could not receive the Permanent Resident Card of the USA. My husband said he would not give me the written permission to take our two children to America, if only I gave him the last chance to restore our family. I did not want to accept his conditions, but my father explained me that I had to do what my ex-husband was asking me to do in order to bring my children to America.

I thought couple of days and then, I agreed with my father. I understood that I did not have the other choice, if I wanted to bring my children with me to the USA. I would never leave them in my native country by themselves. So, I had to accept my ex-husband's offer and I had to come together with him. My ex-husband started calling me very often, asking me to meet with him after that event.

Long story short, we passed all the necessary interviews in my native country and we bought tickets, and we were making plans about how we would live in America.

My husband's all relatives became very nice with me, because all of them asked me to help their families to receive the Green card and to visit America. I informed them that I would not be able to help them with receiving the Green Card of the USA, but I advised them to participate in the lottery Green Card game every year.

This event reminded me about God's Words from the Bible,

where the Most High God told His people that He will make our enemies to come and ask us to help them. Isaiah 60:14 (Bible, New International Version) The children of your oppressors will come bowing before you; all who despise you will bow down at your feet and will call you the City of the LORD, Zion of the Holy One of Israel.

After this event, my husband became nice with our two children and me. I remembered how my mother-in-law asked me, before her death, to help her son to change his work, since she was sure that her son used to work in a stressful job (as a butcher). I promised to my mother-in-law to do my best to help her son to change his job. Almighty God helped him to change his job, when he had to leave to the USA.

After six months, we moved to the USA. My parents met us at the airport. My parents rented one room in their neighbor's apartment and they prepared everything for us to live in that room. They bought a carpet, sofa and the beds for us. So, we started to live in one and the same building with my parents, but in the different apartments.

I was living with my husband as a family, but we could not be happy again. He was always complaining that America was not a good place to live and work. He was always complaining about something to be wrong and bad in our lives. It was very difficult to live with a person, who was always unhappy and complaining that everything was wrong and bad in his life.

I explained to him that every person, who immigrated, would meet some difficulties at the beginning. I told him later we would have a better life. I advised him to sell his meat stores in our native country and to use this money to open a meat store in the USA. So, we would not have to work for somebody, but he never listened to my advices. He did not want to change anything in our lives. He used to be at his work most of the time.

I felt that I should not live with such kind of person like him. I used to take care of our two kids by myself and I used to make all the shopping and laundry for us. My husband used to work and he never spent time for us. I told him many times that we should change our way of living, because he was not spending time for our children and me.

I went to look for a job to different stores, organizations, since I had a fluent English. I did not want to work as a Home Health Aid. I could not find any job during three months.

Later my friend said that she knew a day care center, where I could enroll my children. I went to that day care center and I enrolled my two children there. I wanted my children to be ready for the American Public Schools and to improve their knowledge of English.

In that day care center, I met a young man, who was working at that place as a social worker. He showed us the Day Care Center. He was very kind and sociable person. His name was Alex. My friend told him that I had a good experience of working as a manager in our native country and I had been looking for a job for three months already. Alex sent me to the office, where there was a vacancy for the position of a coordinator. Alex helped me to prepare all the documents, which I needed to show for the first interview.

I went to the interview and the manager liked that I could speak in six languages. They offered me that job. The salary was low, but I agreed to start working at that office as a coordinator.

After couple of weeks Alex and my other friends advised me to open a medical coverage for my children and me, and to see the doctors. I had a good chance to improve my health in America. I went and I opened the medical coverage for my two children, my husband and myself.

I went to a primary doctor and gynecologist, and I found out that I had a third-degree uterine cancer. My gynecologist told me that I had Human Papillomavirus infection, which passed from my husband. She explained me that usually people get HPV from genital contact. I told her that in my native country my husband infected me with a genital transmitted disease several times. I explained to my gynecologist that I tried to get the treatment by drinking many different antibiotics, given by my doctors in my native country. My gynecologist explained me that I needed to have the uterine surgery as soon as possible, if I wanted to live.

I informed my husband about my gynecologist's words and

the surgery. He said he did not want me to receive the surgery, as he wanted to have more children. I asked my parents and my sister about that surgery. Everybody suggested me to have that surgery as soon as possible, except my husband.

I decided to get that surgery, because I wanted to live and take care of my two children. I told the supervisor at my work about that surgery and I took several days off. My friends had heard about the surgery. My husband could not take me to that surgery, since he had to go to his work. He did not want to take a day off from his work at the surgery day.

Alex had heard from our friends about the surgery and he offered to take me to the surgery, and to bring me back after that surgery on his car. I accepted his offer. Alex went with me to that surgery. I was so scared of any surgeries. I told Alex to leave to his job during the surgery, but Alex refused to leave me there.

After the surgery Alex took me back home on his car, because I was very weak after the anesthesia. When I came home, I felt so stressed that my husband did not even call me to know how the surgery had passed. My husband could take the day off and he could support me at the surgery. As usually, my husband never supported me.

My primary doctor sent me to examine my thyroid after couple of weeks. After the doctor's exams and after biopsy of my thyroid, I was told that there might be a cancer in my thyroid. I was informed that I needed to have the surgery of removing the right part of my thyroid. Again cancer! Again surgery! I was stressed out. I agreed to have that surgery. I told to my sister and my parents about the surgery. Nobody could go with me to support me at that surgery, because everybody had to be at his or her work. My husband did not want to take a day off from his work. So, he went to his work that day. I had to go to the surgery by myself. It was so scary for me. I explained to the supervisor that I was going to have a surgery. The supervisor told me to stay home for three weeks after the surgery to be completely recovered.

I went to the hospital in Manhattan. I was sitting and waiting for the doctors to call me, when suddenly I saw Alex coming towards me. I was surprised to see him. He was upset that I did not tell him about that surgery, he said: "a friend in need is a friend indeed". I told him I did not want to bother him, as Alex had to work too. I thanked Alex for supporting me and I asked him to leave. I went to the surgery. The surgery took eight hours. When I opened my eyes, I saw Alex sitting next to my bed. Alex spoke with doctors about me. He was concerned about condition of my health. He felt sorry for me, cause I had the second surgery at that time. I thanked Alex for supporting me and I asked him to live.

I had to spend one night at that hospital. My husband did not even come to visit me after that surgery. The next day, Alex brought me home on his car. We (my parents and me) thanked Alex for his help.

I was so thankful to the USA government that they had paid for my both surgeries and all the medicines, which I had had during those treatments. My medical coverage paid for the night that I spent at the hospital. I am so grateful to the Most High God that He saved me from the death twice. Doctors told me, if I did not have those two surgeries on time, then the cancer could take my life in several months.

In my country I went to the different gynecologists to have a treatment, but they could not treat me. I took a lot of antibiotics in my native country to treat some infections that I was told to treat. But the doctors, in my native country, never told me that I had the HPV infection and I had the uterine cancer of the second degree. If Almighty God did not give me a chance to win the Green Card Lottery Game, I would not be alive since 2010. God of Israel saved my life, by giving me the Permanent Resident Card to enter the USA.

I was one in the couple of millions of people, who had the chance and luck from the Most High God, to win that game and to receive permission to study, live and work in the USA. In America, I received the right treatments. The doctors conducted two surgeries and they saved my life from two cancers. Almighty God saved my life with the help of those doctors and with the help of the USA.

Before I won the Green Card lottery game, I entered the embassy of the USA and asked for the visa to come to America to visit my parents. I was denied the Visa. I was told that the economic and environmental crisis in my native country used to make people of the country to immigrate to other developed countries of the world. Since I was young, the embassy believed that I could stay in the USA and immigrate in there. That is why I could not visit the USA before winning the Green Card Lottery Game.

I want to emphasize that every good thing in my life had happened, because of the Most High God's help.

I recovered from the second surgery in five weeks. I went back to work. The salary, which I was receiving at that office, was not enough to pay all my bills. After all, I wanted to receive a diploma or license in America. I wanted to be a qualified specialist in order to find the job, where I would be paid a good salary to cover my expenses.

I spoke with different people in America and I was advised to study in Master's Degree in Special Education Early Childhood. So, I took the loan and I started to study at Touro College. Then, I wet to the day care center, where my sister had been working with Alex, at that time, and I spoke with the manager, asking for a job of a teacher.

The supervisor called Alex and my sister, because they both had been working at that day care center, and she asked them some questions about me to get some reference. Of course, Alex and my sister told a lot of positive things about me. The supervisor took me for the job of a teacher for the preschoolers. So, I started to work in that day care center with Alex and my sister.

Meanwhile, my husband used to fight with me again, telling the negative and bad things about my parents and me. I did remind him about the help and support of my parents, when we just came to the USA. He acted as if he did not care about that.

Later on, my husband started another fight with me, asking me to give him all the money I earned. He also wanted me to give him the income tax return money. Whatever my husband used to earn, he used to send it to his father and his sisters in our native country. He did not like to spend money for our two children, stating that our children were too young to spend for them money. At that time, my daughter used to attend the kindergarten and my son used to attend the first grade in a Public School of the USA.

I got very tired of such quarrels with my husband and I asked him to leave me alone. I went to a lawyer in the USA and I filed the divorce papers again at the beginning of 2011. We started living separately with my husband. I had less stress and less quarrels at home. I used to go to my work and after work I used to go to the college, where I used to study for my Master's Degree in Special Education.

I asked my husband to give some money every month to spend for our two children, but he refused to assist us with our living expenses. I asked my husband to pay the alimony for our kids, but he refused.

I decided to stop asking him for his help in paying our expenses. I took all the responsibilities on myself. I worked from Monday till Friday and I studied in the evening time. I took care of my two children, taking them to school and picking them up from the school. I did the entire job about the house –cooking, cleaning, shopping and laundry. Of course, my parents were helping me a lot during those days. My parents used to sit with my children, while I had been studying at the College.

But most of all, the Most High God helped me to survive during those days. Almighty God helped me through such people like my parents, my sister and my friends. I had to pass five state exams in order to continue my education at the college. Almighty God even helped me to pass those exams. My friends at my college told me about the different courses that might be helpful during those state exams. I attended those courses. I passed those exams during one and a half year, while some of my friends had a difficult time in passing some of those exams. I always used to see how the Most High God was helping me to solve the problems that I had met at that time.

I used to work at the day care center and my salary was not enough to cover the rent, and food, and all the other expenses that I had, since I was a single parent with two children at that time. I worked really hard for the supervisor to raise my salary as she had promised me, but still my salary was not raised. I used to cry some times, thinking that the money I earned was barely enough to pay all my bills and I could not save anything for the future. Everything that I used to earn, I had to spend to pay my life expenses.

Couple of months later, Almighty God made another miracle in my life. The Day Care Center, where I had been working was closed due to some violations. The next day, I found a job in another day care center, but in the position of a Teacher-Director. My salary became almost twice higher than it had been at the previous day care center. I was so surprised on how God of Israel used the obstacles and the problems in my life to help me; when I lost my job at the first the day care center, the next day, Almighty God gave me the job much better than I had before. I started to work as a Teacher – Director in another day care center.

It is like in Matthew 25:23 from the Bible (English Standard Version) - His master said to him, "Well done, good and faithful servant. You have been faithful over a little; I will set you overmuch. Enter into joy of you master". I had been faithful in the first day care center with a very small salary. Then, the Most High God trusted me the job of a Teacher-Director with a higher salary.

I had been working almost nine months at that day care center. My sister and Alex also used to work with me at the same place. The owners of that day care center were really rude with us – workers. I did not pay attention to that. Later on, the owners used to bring food products, which were expired, to cook for the children of that day care center.

I spoke with the owners and I told them that as a director I would not allow the cooker to use expired products for kid's food. The owners told me that I was just a director and I had to do what they asked me to. I did not agree with them. I resigned from my job of a Teacher- Director, because I knew that children might get sick from the expired food. Alex and my sister also left their job for the same reason.

I called all the parents and I informed them about the expired food in that day care center. I also told them that I was not working at that day care center any more, because I could not participate in such actions against the children. I also went to the Health Department and I informed them about that. I was sure that as a teacher I had to inform all the necessary departments, who used to protect children's rights.

Later, I had heard from the parents, whose children used to attend that day care center, that two children had been taken to the hospital by their parents, after being poisoned from the expired food. Health Department came to check the day care center and they found the expired milk and eggs in refrigerator.

The new Teacher -Director was in a trouble at that time. I thanked the Most High God that I was not working at the day care center during those violations.

I started to file an application to open my own Group Family Day Care center. It took almost nine months to receive the license for the Group Family Day Care Center. Alex used to help me in filing all the necessary documents.

During those two years, I had been working with Alex. One day he told me that he fell in love with me. I did not even think about that, when we used to work together. Alex really helped me a lot during those years. From the first day, when I met him, Alex used to help me. He used to drive us to the hospitals, when we needed. My son had a crack on his right ankle twice. Alex used to bring us to the hospital and to the Pediatric Orthopedist, when we needed.

My ex-husband used to call me all those years, asking me to forgive him. I forgave him, but I did not want to live with him anymore. I knew the fact that my ex-husband used to have the other women on the side besides me. I did not want to live with such kind of man anymore. That is why I did not want to live with him anymore. Our children did not want to live with their biological father either. My children told me that their biological father never took care of them and they knew the fact that their biological father gave me the sickness. They also remembered how their biological father used to make the quarrels at home a lot. My children knew Alex already, as they used to attend the day care center, where he had worked before. My children told me that they preferred to live with Alex rather than with their biological father. Since, I informed them and I asked their point of views about getting married with Alex.

Almost two years, I was confused in my personal life questions. I did not know what to do. I had two ways to continue my life. The first way - was to live with my ex-husband, with whom I had divorced already. The second way - was to agree to marry with Alex and to create a new family with him. I was confused very much. I prayed to Almighty God, asking Him to help me to make the right choice.

My ex-husband heard about Alex and about his love to me. One day, Alex met with my ex-husband and told him to leave me alone, because we were divorced already. Alex told him he wanted to marry me and he wanted to create a family with me.

I decided to give myself some time to make the right decision in my life. I called Alex and I told him that I would give one more chance to my ex-husband and I would live with him. I asked Alex to find another woman to marry. Alex left to his native country for several months to take care of his father.

At the same time, I told my ex-husband I would never live with him again and I asked him to find another wife to marry with.

I decided to be alone and find out what my heart would tell me about my personal life questions.

When Alex left, I understood that I fell in love with him. I understood that I could not live without Alex. Still, I was not sure, if the Most High God wanted me to live with Alex instead of my ex-husband.

Alex came back from his native country. One day, he called me very late at night and told me that he wanted to show me very important thing about my ex-husband. I decided to go with Alex and see. When we came to a Dunking donuts, I saw my ex-husband, sitting with another young woman and drinking tea or coffee. It was at 12:15 am at midnight.

I went inside the Dunking Donuts place and I spoke with them both. I looked at my ex-husband and I said to him to be happy with her and not to follow me anymore. He left the young woman and ran after me. I came home and I did not speak with my ex-husband that day. I did not answer his phone calls too. He tried to speak with me, and explain something to me. I just sent him the text message, telling him to go back to the woman and to be happy with her.

My ex-husband kept following me, trying to live with our children and me. I decided to change my address. I moved to another apartment in order to avoid my ex-husband's pressure on me. I did not tell him my new address.

In the bottom of my heart, I was scared to go to the unknown future. As for me, it would be easier to forgive my ex-husband and live with him, instead of living with Alex. Like a habit, I was thinking to forgive my ex-husband and live with him. I told Alex that I would forgive my ex-husband and live with him, because he was the biological father of my two children. Alex went to his native country again, since his father was very sick and Alex had to take care of his father.

One day, I was sitting in the park with my children, when my ex-husband came to talk with me. He found our new address and us. I was surprised to see him in the park at that time. I spoke with him and I, suddenly, remembered that many years ago, I had asked the Most High God to give me "the husband" from Almighty God. I realized that I did not want to live with my ex-husband anymore. I forgave my ex-husband, but I did not love him and I did not want to live with him anymore. I told my ex-husband to find a nice wife and to marry her. I told him it was my final answer. He left me, thinking that I would give up and live with him again. He was sure that I would come one day and I would live with him again, like I used to do in my native country, when I used to forgive him after his each betrayal.

After couple of days, Alex started texting me from his native country. I did not answer his text messages, because I wanted to be alone and I wanted to find out what my heart wanted. I used to pray all the time, asking Almighty God to help me to make the right decision in my life. I wanted the Most High God to make that choice for me, instead of me. I was thinking and analyzing again and again. It was very difficult for me to accept the changes in my life. I was feeling the great fear of the changes in my life. I was scared to make a choice.

One day, I was praying as I used to do once a day. Suddenly, when I asked the Most High God to give me the happiness in my life, I had heard the strong voice in the bottom of my heart. That voice told me: "You asking me to give you the happiness, then why are you trying to interrupt me? If you want to be happy, then let me make you happy. You are not letting me to give you the happiness you asking me." I said to my heart: "God, how did I interrupt you from making me happy?" I received the answer right away. That voice in my heart said: "If you want to be happy, then do not try to live with your ex-husband. I was trying to separate you from him in your native country, by letting him infect you with genital transmitted diseases several times. Still you used to live with your ex-husband again and again. I gave you the different signs to stop living with your ex-husband, but you have never heard me. I sent some people telling you not to live with your ex-husband in your native country; still you used to ignore the words of those people. You are always scared to rely your life and your future on Me. If you choose to live with your ex-husband, and if you continue living with your ex-husband, I will take your life. I gave you many diseases as the sings to leave that person and to build your life without him; you still afraid to

75

live your life without your ex-husband. But I will never let you live with your ex-husband. If you decide to live with him, you will never be happy."

I started to weep from the happiness, as the Most High God answered my questions and directed me to the right choice, which I had to make. I did not want to make the choice that would be against the Most High God's will.

In several weeks, Alex came back from his native country. He called me, and he asked me to be with him and marry him. I agreed and I accepted his proposal. Meanwhile, my ex-husband used to call me, asking me to meet with him. I told my ex-husband that I made up my mind and I was marrying Alex. My ex-husband called Alex and asked him to meet with him. Alex went to see him one more time. They spoke and my ex-husband called me, being next to Alex. I said to him that I loved Alex and I decided to live with Alex. My ex-husband got very upset.

I understood that I had passed some tests from the Most High God. I was so happy that Almighty God helped me to find the way out from that "fearful" situation, in which I had been for a long time. I got married with Alex and we went to travel for two weeks to Brazil. We visited Saint Christ the Redeemer. This statue is located at the peak of the 700-metre Corcovado Mountain in the Tijuca Forest National Park overlooking the city of Rio de Janeiro.

We went up to that Monument. I was so happy, because

the Most High God gave me a chance to visit such a wonderful place that was dedicated to Jesus Christ. I was so happy that I had a chance to have a pilgrimage to the monument, dedicated to Jesus Christ.

We came back to the USA and we started to work in our own Group Family Day Care Center. I had been working as the On-site Provider with Alex and my Mother. We were (are) living happily with Alex.

I understood that Almighty God had heard my words and gave me the "Husband from the Most High God", because Alex used to take care of me very much. Alex used to respect me and appreciate me the way I had been. Alex used to tell the other people that he was so proud to have such wife like me. In one words, Alex became such husband that I was dreaming about and asking Almighty God about. I remembered how eleven years ago, I asked the Most High God, if He could give me the "Husband from Him (God)", who would love me the way I was; the husband, who would treat me respectfully; the husband, who would appreciate my work and me; the husband, who would not complain all the time, telling me I was a bad woman; the husband, who would not tell bad and negative things about my parents and relatives.

God did keep His promise to me. As the Most High God told me in one of my Dreams seven years ago the following words:

Isaiah 41:10 (Bible, New Living Translation) " Don't fear,

because I am with you; don't be afraid, for I am Your God. I will strengthen you, I will surely help you; I will hold you with my righteous strong hand." (Bible New American Standard Bible) Psalm 91:9 " For you have made the LORD, my refuge, Even the Most High, your dwelling place. " (Psalm 91:10) No evil will befall you, Nor will any plague come near your tent. (Psalm 91:11) For He will give His angels charge concerning you, To guard you in all your ways. (Psalm 91:12) They will bear you up with their hands, That you do not strike your foot against a stone. (Psalm 91:13) You will tread upon the lion and the cobra; The young lion and the serpent you will trample underfoot. (Psalm 91:14) Because he has loved Me, I will deliver him; I will set him securely on high, because he has known My Name. (Psalm 91:15) He will call upon Me, and I will answer him; I will be with him in trouble; I will rescue him and honor him. (Psalm 91:16) With a long life I will satisfy him And let him see My salvation."

Those words God told in my Vision, when my ex-husband's mother was passing away. During couple of minutes, I fell sleep and I saw that dream, and I had heard those words.

I wrote this Book about my life to show and prove the people that God of Israel is Real, and God is Alive, and the Most High God is taking care of all his children. In my Book, I used the events from my life and my Dreams, when the Most High God spoke with me, informing me how to live in order to show the people, who would read this book that we need to live relying only on God (God of Israel). We need to read the Bible every day in order to protect ourselves from sins, which would bring the sickness, loneliness, and destruction, and even death into our lives. As soon as I started to read the Bible, many miracles took place in my life. So, if you want the Most High God to change your life, and to help you to reach your goals and dreams, then read the BIBLE.

God showed me His power by giving me one more chance to live in this world when:

1. I was healed from two cancers;
2. I moved to the USA;
3. I continued my education in the USA, as I dreamed;
4. I met the real "Husband from the Most High God", who really loves me.
5. I have wonderful, smart, cute son and daughter.

God showed me His power. As it is written in the Bible:

Revelation 21:4 (Bible, New International Version)" He will wipe away every tear from their eyes. There will be no more death or mourning or crying or pain, for the old order of things has passed away".

Now, you can see through my life, how the Most High God – the Creator of the Universe- gave me the second chance to live. Almighty God changed my life in such a way, when I forgot every wrong thing that had happened to me before. I forgot all the pains and hurts, which I had had. I met the new people. I started to live in a new way. I started to live in the way I wanted to live, and in the way I dreamed to live. God of Israel even gave me the people, who supported me, respected me; and the people, who loved me the way I was.

2 Corinthians 3:18 (Bible, New American Standard Bible) But we all, with unveiled face, beholding as in a mirror the glory of the Lord, are being transformed into the same image from glory to glory, just as from the Lord, the Spirit. I can connect these sentences from the Bible with my life, when the Most High God improved my life, and brought us higher and higher all the time (from glory to glory).

The Most High God even had heard our praying and helped my only brother to move to the USA. My brother had been living alone in our native country for several years. Then, my brother went to Moscow to work there in a pharmacy.

My brother had a liver surgery in our native country. After that surgery, my brother got the disease - Hepatitis C. My brother tried to get the necessary medicines in our native country, but he could not. Later, he tried to get those medicines and treatments in Moscow, but it was very expensive. We could not afford to pay all the treatments, he needed.

My Mother and me, we used to pray a lot, asking the Most High God to help my brother to move to the USA and receive the necessary treatments, and the medicines in here. Since we knew that in the USA people could get treatments they needed. Even though, when the people could not afford to pay those treatments, the government of the USA would support them, and would pay for them through different medical coverage.

I was sure that Almighty God would bring my brother into the USA, because I saw a Dream about that. I always used to tell my Mother not to worry about my brother, because the Most High God had showed me in my Vision that He would help my brother to come to the USA. I always used to inform my relatives about that dream. In that Vision, Jesus Christ showed me how the negative people, surrounding us, could affect us; how the demons could get inside of our brains through our eyes, when we see something bad (the things that make us sin). The demons would get inside of our brains, and they would control our lives and actions. Jesus held my right hand and took me to the Hell. I saw how people suffered in the Hell. Jesus was explaining me and showing me, how the demons were getting inside of the brains of the people, using their eyes and controlling their lives, and behaviors. Jesus showed me how the demons were hurting people and how they were destroying their lives.

Then, Jesus took me to the Heaven. I did not remember how we got there. Jesus took my right hand and I opened my eyes, and I was in the Heaven with my two children. In the Heaven, I had been sitting and playing with my children and there had been a lot of other children, playing and having fun. There was no sun in that place. Even though, that place was so bright and the brightness was so powerful. I did not see the Most High God, but I had heard His voice talking to me. The Creator of the Universe– Almighty God - told me: "Be aware and careful about your children's friends and the people surrounding your kids. Your children's friends would affect, where your children would spend there eternity in the Heaven (Paradise) or in the Hell. If your children make friends with wrong people, then those people would attract your children and teach them wrong things to do (to sin). If your children become friends with positive, nice, generous people, then your children would learn to live properly, according to My principles of life, escaping the sins."

As soon as the Most High God told me those words, I saw my brother coming and standing at this place with me, in the Heaven. My brother was so happy, calm, and satisfied with his life. When I saw my brother, I became very happy. I told my brother to look at that wonderful place. I told him to pay attention on how that place was bright and peaceful.

After that Vision, I became sure that Almighty God would help my brother to come to the USA in God's determined time. I used to inform my Mother and other relatives that we should not worry, but we should rely all our problems on God of Israel. Since the Most High God showed us already, that He would bring my brother to the USA and would heal him from the Hepatitis C.

Five years passed after that Dream, when my brother came to the USA from Moscow. Everybody in our family and all our relatives from my native country could not believe in the fact that my brother moved to the USA, without anybody's help. He moved to the USA with the Most High God's help only. It was a miracle in my brother's life. Nobody helped him, except the Creator of the Universe– Almighty God. Still, people are wondering how a young man – my brother - could get a permission to enter the USA. Because in our native country, it was almost impossible to get the permission to enter the USA, being at such young age as thirty-four years old.

When my brother came to the USA, he applied for the permanent green card to the immigration service. My brother sent all the necessary applications to the immigration service. After couple of months, my brother was granted a medical coverage. He went to the hospital. My brother received the necessary treatments and medicines from the hospital to treat the Hepatitis C. My brother was fully healed from that dangerous disease during almost 10 months. The Government covered all the treatments, cause my brother had a medical coverage and he did not have a high income at that time.

I want to write about the endless power of Almighty God – the Creator of the Universe. There is nothing impossible for the

Creator of the Universe. My Heavenly Father treated me from the two cancers. Then, the Most High God treated my brother from the Hepatitis C as well. Almighty God gave us the chance to live and serve other people, surrounding us.

When I prayed, I used to ask the Most High God to help my ex-husband to find his love and his happiness. After several months, I had heard from our friends that my ex-husband married and he had a happy life with his second family.

We need to forgive our enemies and the people, who treated us wrong; and the people, who hurt us. We need to pray for our enemies. I did those things, which Almighty God asked me to do about my enemies. The Most High God punished every person in my life, who treated me wrong and did hurt me in the past. I still pray for those people, asking God of Israel to forgive them.

My father-in-law passed away, being and living alone in our native country. He was very sick during the last days of his life. My father-in-law threatened me to kill me with his dark magic. As a result, the Most High God took his life, when my father-in-law was only 66 years old. The Most High God put all my enemies very far away from me. Thanks to Almighty God, I did not see those people (my enemies) anymore. As we can read in the Bible (New International Version):

Isaiah 41:12. "Though you search for your enemies, you

will not find them. Those who wage war against you will be as nothing at all.

Isaiah 41:13. For I am the LORD your God who takes hold of your right hand and says to you, Do not fear; I will help you.

Isaiah 41:14. Do not be afraid, you worm Jacob, little Israel, do not fear, for I myself will help you," declares the LORD, your Redeemer, the Holy One of Israel.

Isaiah 41:16. You will winnow them, the wind will pick them up, and a gale will blow them away. But you will rejoice in the LORD and glory in the Holy One of Israel.

Isaiah 41:17. The poor and needy search for water, but there is none; their tongues are parched with thirst. But I the LORD will answer them; I, the God of Israel, will not forsake them.

Isaiah 41:18. I will make rivers flow on barren heights, and springs within the valleys. I will turn the desert into pools of water, and the parched ground into springs.

Isaiah 41:19. I will put in the desert the cedar and the acacia, the myrtle and the olive. I will set junipers in the wasteland, the fir and the cypress together,

Isaiah 41:20. So that people may see and know, may consider and understand, that the hand of the LORD has done this, that the Holy One of Israel has created it.

Malachi 3:11. I will prevent pests from devouring your crops, and the vines in your fields will not drop their fruit before it is ripe," says the LORD Almighty.

Malachi 3:12. " Then all the nations will call you blessed, for yours will be delightful land," says the LORD Almighty.

Malachi 4:2. But for you who revere My Name, the sun of righteousness will rise with healing in its rays. And you will go out and frolic like well-fed calves.

"Deuteronomy 7:15 (Bible, English Standard Version)– And LORD will take away from you all sickness, and none of the evil diseases of Egypt, which you knew, will He inflict on you, but He will lay them on all who hate you". I can connect those words from the Bible with the period of my life, when I had been living in the family of my ex-husband. My ex-husband's family and his house had been the Egypt for me at that time. When I was in their "slavery". All of my ex-husband's relatives used to treat me very rudely and disrespectfully most of the time.

Our enemies cannot defeat us, if we know that Almighty God is Our Heavenly Father, Provider and Vindicator. The favor of God will keep our enemies from defeating us.

We need to remember that Almighty God will pay us back for the unfair things that have happened to us. Almighty God always ends in all His Wells. Our God will take what meant for our harm and use it to our advantage. We need to keep a good attitude, when it is not fair. When we keep doing the right things, when the wrong things are happening - the favor of God in our lives will cause us to rise above every difficulty.

My life is happened to be the proving example of those words, mentioned above. The Most High God took everything that was meant to hurt me and He used it to my advantage. When people destroyed my relationship with my ex-husband, I had to divorce. The Most High God gave me the right person, who made me happy. I met the person, who appreciates me, respects me, and loves me. God of Israel paid me back for the unfair situations that had happened to me. It took place, when the Most High God healed me from the two cancers and I moved with my children to the country, where I dreamed to live (the USA).

I dreamed to study in America and Almighty God gave me such chance – I graduated the Master's Degree Special Education Early Childhood in the USA.

The Most High God helped me to reach my dreams. The only thing I had to do is to do the right things, when the wrong things were happening to me. I did my best to follow and keep in my life Almighty God's principles and rules of living. I learned those principles and rules of life from the Bible. I do advice every person in this world to read the Bible every day, little by little and to follow all the Principles of the Most High God.

When I read the Bible, I hear God's words and advices towards my life. I think that there is nothing more important and valuable in this world than Almighty God's words to us – the words of the Creator of the Universe.

As a result, I can underline the following principles that

every person should follow during his/her life in order to reach the huge successes in their lives:

1) Never take revenge on your enemies. Only God has that right – the right to avenge your enemies.

2) Go forward without looking to your past. Look forward and go to your Dreams. Do your Best to reach your Dreams and the Most High God will do for you those things that you are not able to do.

3) Rely only on God. Do not rely on people and on people's help. Trust God every second of your life. Trust God in every sphere of your life.

4) Whatever was meant for your harm, Almighty God will take it and change it for your good. Whatever it could be.

5) Read the Bible and talk to the people about the Most High God, and everything that God of Israel gave you, and did in your life. Tell the people how God changed your life and how God helped you to overcome the obstacles in your life.

6) Accept Jesus as your Savior and follow all His Principles to live without a sin.

7) Do not go to the fortune-tellers ever. If we need an advise in our lives, first of all, we should ask God's help and His advise for our problems. While we pray, we need to ask the Most High God's guidance in every sphere of our lives. We need to say "Thank you God" beforehand.

The king Saul was punished by Almighty God very badly, when Saul went to the fortune-teller and asked her about his future. Bible, New Living Translation:

1 Chronicles 10:13. So Saul died for he was unfaithful to the LORD. He failed to obey the LORD's command, and he even consulted a medium for guidance

1 Chronicles 10:14 instead of asking the LORD for guidance. So the LORD killed him and turned the kingdom over to David the son of Jesse.

God punished me too, for asking the guidance from a fortune-teller. Alex wanted to start a new business with the foreigners. We went to a fortune-teller to ask her advice and to know, if we could trust those foreign businessmen. Almost six months later, I saw a Dream (Vision), where I had heard the voice from the sky telling me: "You went to the fortune-teller, asking for her guidance in your life, so now you will see what I will bring into your life and you will see the Power of My Anger." I understood that the voice belonged to the Most High God. I got really scared. Then, I saw the blue clean water that washed away everything around me in my Dream. That water rose very high, so it could wash away everything around me and me too, together with my family. The water did not hurt my family and me in my dream.

Several months later, I got pregnant and (Alex and me) we wanted that child very much. In three months, I lost that child.

It was very hard and painful for me. I was pregnant and the child did not develop after three months of my pregnancy. As a result, I lost my child that I dreamed about, and I was sure that the child was a baby boy.

Later, I understood that God of Israel punished me for the fortune-teller that I visited. We should never go to a fortune-teller and ask her/him the questions about our lives or future. If we have a question about our lives, we need to ask the Most High God to help us to find the answers for those questions in our praying. God will help us to solve every problem in our lives. I learnt a very good lesson from the Most High God. I am thankful to Almighty God that He taught me that lesson, because I will never repeat that sin again. I will never go to any fortune-tellers.

8) We need to obey the Most High God in everything He asks us to obey. If the Most High God asks us to let go some people from our lives, we should let him or her go. If we do not obey God, then we will be punished for our disobedience, cause not obeying the LORD is a "huge" sin.

9) We need to trust the LORD in every situation of our lives.

Now, I want to share the following advises that I have received from the Most High God. I believe that following advises will help you to become a winner in your life and to find your place, and happiness in this world. Amen.

1. Do not be in a hurry, when you are doing something.

2. Everything that happens in our lives is for our good.

3. Do not worry of anything in your life. Do not worry of any problem in your life. Almighty God already has the solution to every problem you may have. Even before you were born, God already had the plan for your life and all the solutions to every problem you may (or would) have.

4. "I will protect all my children. I will protect you as well, cause you are my child." - says the Most High God. Amen.

5. Live and work with smile, and in a splendid mood. Live and work being happy, feeling yourself happy as you have Almighty God's love - your Heavenly Father's Love.

6. Never leave for tomorrow what can be done today. Do not be lazy. Laziness is the sin that destroys the happiness in your future. Complete all your works on time.

7. "Rely Only on Me!"- Says God of Israel. Jeremiah 17:7 "But blessed is the one who trusts in the LORD, whose confidence is in Him". Amen.

8. Everything is possible together with the Most High God. There is nothing impossible for Our God - Your Heavenly Father. Amen.

9. Never forget who the Most High God is for you - Your Heavenly Father. Never forget whose you are - You are the Child of Almighty God.

10. Do not forget who you are for God in this world. You are of very great importance for the Most High God.

11. The Most High God knows everything you do or you think, beforehand.

12. Rely only on Almighty God. God will arrange, and put every single thing or a necessary person on the right place of your life, because you are of great importance for your Heavenly Father - Almighty God.

13. Trust all your problems on the Most High God and trust yourself to God. God of Israel will never betray you. Amen.

14. Whatever you are doing, do it as if you are doing it for God - Your Heavenly Father. Do your work with all your heart. God will bless you for that. Amen.

15. Live increasing your faith to God. Have the very strong believe on God.

16. Pay a great attention to the very small details in your life and in every sphere of your life. As those details can tell you God's words and directions towards you and your life (your future).

17. God's eyes are on you every single second of your life, even when you sleep, you smile or cry. The Most High

God has you in the Palm of His Powerful Hands. God will take care of you every second of your life. Amen.

18. The Most High God will show you His Power and Glory through Your life, by using your life. Amen.

19. Live dreaming of the Highest Dreams for Your life. Dream Big, cause your God is the Creator of the Universe and there is no limits to Almighty God's Power. Amen.

20. Your life belongs to God - Your Heavenly Father. Since God had His Plan for you in His "Book of Life", even before you were born. God's Plan for Your life is for good not for evil. Nobody can stop God's plan for you, but you. Remember that. Only you can stop God's plan for you.

21. Never put the borders around yourself. If you do so, you will try to put the borders around God's assistance to your life.

22. Don not live looking at other people, because you are not like the others. You have – Powerful, Almighty, Heavenly Father - the Most High God on your side, who loves you and takes care of you every time. Live looking Only at God - Your Heavenly Father. Go through your life together with God of Israel.

23. God is with you, in every second of your life. The Most High God will never let you fall down. Amen.

24. Whatever happens to you and your life, Almighty God will change it all and everything into the success to you.

The Most High God will bring those obstacles back to you as the success. Cause there is nothing impossible for God - Your Heavenly Father. Amen.

25. Follow all the Principles that Almighty God gave you and live relying on those Principles. Since those Principles will change you, your life and character. You will find those Principles in the Bible, because the Author of the Bible is Almighty God. Amen.

26. You will find the answers to every single question that you may have in the Bible. Read the Bible daily and, while reading it, ask the Most High God your questions. Almighty God will answer all your questions in His way and time, using everything surrounding you - Nature, Animals, Birds and People. Remember that you will find the true answers from the Creator of the Universe, who created everything.

27. God's Love to You will never end. Amen.

28. Never afraid of anything but of sin. Be as far from sin as possible. A sin brings every bad thing in a person's life: sickness, bad luck, quarrel, loneliness, and even death etc.

29. Almighty God loves all His children. Every child of Almighty God is of the same value for God (of great importance).

30. Money should not be the aim of your life. Money should be the source (means) that helps you to reach your Goals. You can bless people with the money.

31. Everyday, look outdoors and wait for the very special Present from your Heavenly Father. Feel and smell, and look for the signs of the gift from the Most High God.

32. Every event has its own time and place to happen. You should know that everything happens in its time and place. You will gather and collect the fruits of your seeds (work) on the time determined by the Most High God-Your Heavenly Father. Be patient.

33. Your Patience, strong Faith, Believe, and Your hard working will lead you to the Success. This is the way to reach the Victory.

34. Protect your Heart all the time, since the strength to live and the happiness flows from your Heart.

35. Do not worry of any problems and obstacles you may have, but ask Almighty God -Your Heavenly Father- in praying with thankfulness, whatever you need and your wishes. Have the very strong faith, the Most High God will answer for your praying and He will give you everything you need in its time.

36. Every time live by learning God's character, seeking His will and His guidelines.

37. Every time live by looking at Your Heavenly Father, looking for His way for your life. Do not look at how other people live, since you are not like them.

38. Be aware of your enemies. Our enemy (devil) never sleeps and it waits for the time to hurt us, and destroy our lives. We may protect ourselves from the enemy ONLY by praying to Our Almighty and the Most High God. If we declare that God is our Shelter, and if we live relying on God, then God will protect us from every negative thing in our lives. The Most High God will turn every negative situation of our lives into the success to us. This life is a war between the devil and us. Fight with our enemy (devil), but not with the people or problems. Our enemy uses the people and obstacles from our lives to ruin our mood, righteousness, family and our entire lives. Try to be strong as much as you can.

39. God of Israel will lift us with the Holy Spirit. Almighty God will change our lives and us, by improving our character. God will make us stronger and wiser. Amen.

40. Every time, when you pray, ask the Most High God to give you His wisdom - not wisdom of the people, but God's wisdom. Only God's wisdom can make us smarter and will help us to make the right decisions in our lives. Only God's wisdom can bring us into the place in this

world, where we can reach our highest potentials and success.

41. Every time, when you pray, ask Almighty God to give you and your relatives His stored up Blessings. And do not forget to tell "Thank you God" in advance. Before you get those Blessings, you need to say "Thank you God" and you should believe, and imagine that you already have those things in reality.

42. Live being strongly concentrated on the main goals of your life. Do not let the routine of that life distract you from the highest goals for your life (your dreams).

43. Every day, remind yourself and other people, who surround you, that everything in this life will be more than just beautiful and marvelous. Our Heavenly Father-Almighty God is the guarantee for us (His children). Amen.

44. Every time take care of your body and health. Take care of your spirit, mood and health. Save your nerves from the stress, relying on Almighty God and thinking about God's Power. Visit the doctors on time. Take care of your health.

45. Be very patient for every dream that you have, because everything in our lives happens in its time. Amen.

46. Live being directed by your spirit, but not by your feelings. You will receive the wisdom from the Most High God in your Spirit. Amen.

47. Do not make a mess from your life, by bringing wrong people into your life, by developing negative thoughts in your mind, and by making different sins during your life.

48. Let go far away from you towards God all your problems, because you cannot solve any of your problems without God's help. Let go from you towards God of Israel the people, who want to leave you. The roles of those people finished in your life. That also means that those people are not allowed by the Most High God to go with you to the places, where you are going. Amen.

49. God's Plan for your life is perfect and it is much better than your own plan for your life. Because the Most High God sees your future and He knows, what is the best for your happiness and future. You need to trust Almighty God 1000% in every choice of your life. What you are thinking to be your happiness might become unhappiness for you in future. God of Israel knows better, what might be for good or for bad for you in your life. Amen.

50. Together with God's help we need to share our happiness with other people, surrounding us - our relatives, friends and etc. Amen.

51. The Most High God will revenge your offenders upon you for all the hurt, pains and injustices you had because of those people. Declare God - Your Heavenly Father - to be your Vindicator. Then, God will be your Vindicator. Amen.

52. Declare Almighty God to be your Provider, Vindicator, Director, and your Shelter in this life. Amen.

53. If you want to be happy then - stop thinking only about yourself. The person, who thinks and lives only for himself or herself, will never be happy. The Most High God created us to serve each other, by helping each other and taking care of the people around us. Almighty God made every single person different from each other. Every person is unique in the way he or she was created by God.

54. You do not know God's power and his strength yet. You cannot even imagine how Powerful and Strong and Almighty is our Heavenly Father - Our God- Our Provider and Vindicator. If you knew at least 10% of God's ability and His power you would never be worried of anything in your life.

55. God of Israel loves you very much and very truly, and sincerely. God's Love towards you will never end. Since you accepted Jesus Christ as Son of God and Your Redeemer and your Lord - nothing can separate you from God's Love. Amen.

56. The Most High God approves everything that you are doing. He says: "How splendid are things and works that you are doing. The seed that you already had planted will bring wonderful fruits very soon. The trees that you planted already have the flowers growing and smelling sweet." Amen.

57. Have the very deep and sincere relation with Almighty God - Your Heavenly Father. Try to hear His voice inside of your heart as often as you can.

58. All the time, go forward in your life. Do not look back, because it belongs to the Most High God already. Trust and believe in the plan that Almighty God has already for your life.

59. Forgive all your offenders and forget all the pains they had caused you. Only God of Israel has the right to revenge. We do not have the right to revenge for ourselves. It is better to give that right and choice to the Most High God. Just think about the difference between your revenge and Almighty God's revenge, the difference between your punishment and God's punishment. Let Almighty God be your Vindicator. God's punishment is very hard, painful, fair and true. Remember God's words to be good to our enemies and offenders, and pray for them. Do what Almighty God asks you to do. This is how we show our trust on God. You should wish the happiness to all

your offenders and then, you will see how God will lift you above those people, who hurt you. Then, you will see God's Power and Glory in Your life. Almighty God said that everybody can do good things to their friends, but not everybody can forgive their enemies and wish them good luck, and happiness and pray for them. Because of that choice we make, the Most High God will reward us - for our trust on God of Israel and our forgiveness. Amen.

60. Be sincere with yourself and everybody. The Most High God is God of the Truth. Almighty God wants you to be and act like him. Do not lie to the people, surrounding you and to yourself.

61. Do not ask people to give you the "Love" that they do not have. People cannot give you the real "Love" that you need in this life. Since, only the Most High God has the "True and Real Love" towards us – His children. Only God loves us sincerely. Only Almighty God loves us the way we want to be loved and appreciated.

62. Do not ask the people to give you those things that they do not have.

63. Remember, no one can take away from you the people and all the things that Almighty God gave you. If the Most High God connects and joins two people - no one should destroy their relationship.

64. Whatever is stolen from you by Devil (Whatever it may be? It may be your happiness, your marriage, children and things you dreamed about) – the Most High God will return them back to you, increased for many times, if you rely on God, by giving and trusting Him your life. Amen.

65. Remind yourself every single day the following words of the Most High God: "Success will follow you in all your beginnings." Almighty God already blessed everything that you are doing or you are planning to do. Amen.

66. Everything will happen in its time and place, as it is written and planned in God's "Book of Life". Amen.

67. Your Heavenly Father – God of Israel says to you: "Trust me from the very bottom of your heart, every single second of your life ". We need to trust the Most High God and then, we need to do good things to other people.

68. During your life, you will receive those things that you are expecting to receive. What you are expecting from your life - you will receive it. If you expect to receive small things in your life, then you will receive those small things. If you expect "Big" things from Almighty God, then God will give you those "Big dreams".

69. Belief is expecting what you want to receive from your life. So, try to believe only in the happiness and in all the best for your life. You should trust on the huge dreams

for your life. You should expect the huge gifts from the Most High God.

70. What was stolen from you in your life will be returned to you by Almighty God, in its determined time. Amen.

71. Save and improve all the grants (gifts) that you have at that particular time of your life. (Your ability to walk, speak, your eyes, hands etc.).

72. Respect and value those people surrounding you. Do not take them for granted. They are your spouse, children, parents, relatives, friends, neighbors, co-workers and other people you live and work with, you study together; the people, whom Almighty God put in your life for some purpose.

73. Almighty God will lift you, by giving you and your family a success, and good health. God will show you the things and places you have never seen before. Amen.

74. Your offenders will come and ask you for your help and assistance in their lives, in the time and place determined by the Most High God. Amen.

75. Your Heavenly Father- Almighty God - is hearing every word that you are saying to God, when you pray. God is looking at every single thing that you are doing in your life.

76. Your happiness is right ahead of you. You should go forward to your happiness and take it or reach it. If it did

not work, then take the other thing and try it, until you find your real happiness in this life.

77. All the time remind yourself that you are a good person in this huge world. You should also remember that you are good not because of who you are, but because of whose you are - YOU ARE CHILD OF ALMIGHTY GOD. Amen.

78. Who you are is not determined by how you perform or act in this world. Who you are is determined, by who your Heavenly Father is. Whatever you reach in your life - you reach with the help of Your Heavenly Father - the Most High God. Amen.

79. Follow your Dreams. Live for your Dreams. Remember – your Talents will bring a success into your life. We have only one chance to live in this wonderful world. So, do not waste your life for the problems and routine of this world, but live for the dreams that God put in your heart. Try to improve your gifts from Almighty God - Your Heavenly Father- in many different ways. Try to use your gifts and improve them during your journey in this life.

80. Remember - Your Best Days are ahead of you. You have not seen the Best days of your life that God has in His Store for you and your family. Amen.

81. Almighty God will take you to the places you have not been before and to the places you did not even imagine. Amen.

82. The Most High God - Your Heavenly Father - wants you to live large, happy, abundant and fulfilled life. You need to dream Big, think Big, believe in Big and expect large life in order to reach that kind of life. You cannot think small, believe in small, expect small and, then receive a large life. Our lives are large, but many people are still living in a small way, because they believe in small dreams.

83. You have to change the way of your thinking, believing and expecting. Then, and only then, your life will be changed into Big and Large life with the huge success in it. Amen.

84. Before telling or pronouncing any word or a sentence stop and remind yourself that every word, said by you or by the people surrounding you, will become true. Remember, before the creation of that World, God of Israel said and ordered for everything to happen and to be, and then, everything became reality and true. Every God's word became true. Since, we were created in the image of Our Heavenly Father – the Creator of the Universe - we have the ability to tell and order to the things to happen in our lives.

85.  Declare everyday the success, happiness, healing and God's Blessings above your life and the lives of the people, surrounding you. Amen.

86.  Do not become friends with every single person you meet in your life. Choose the people, with whom you will become friends. I am not talking about the people with whom you work, but I mean the people, with whom you spend your free time. The people you spend time with will either improve your life or destroy it. Remember that chickens live and have fun with the chickens, and the eagles usually fly by themselves. Be friends with noble, righteous and successful people to become like them - smart, generous and successful. Amen.

87.  Follow the steps that Your Heavenly Father is showing you. Feel it and follow Almighty God's way, and principles during your journey. Amen.

88.  Try to live in this world reducing the stress, which will come across your life and the lives of other people surrounding you. You can reach it, only when you rely every single problem of your life - on the Most High God.

89.  Be comfortable and thankful for how Almighty God created you and made you. Appreciate and improve the gifts and grants, which God gave you. All the time, tell to yourself: "I am good. Almighty God made me good. Thank You God for the person you made me. Amen."

90.  You should seek the Most High God every day from the early morning. You should do your Best to please Your Heavenly Father – Almighty God- by following God's principles and rules of living. If you do these steps, you should know and be sure for 1000% that Huge Rewards are coming towards you from the Most High God - Your Provider and Vindicator. You should expect those Huge Wonderful Grants and Rewards From Almighty God and you should be ready to receive them. If you are seeking God with all your heart, and if you are following Almighty God's principles, and you are reading the Bible, then you should be ready to receive Rewards from the Most High God in the time determined by God.

91.  Keep the Most High God in the first place of your life every time. The main goal of your life should not be the money and earning money - but your main goal should be to honor the Most High God every single time you are able to do during your journey. Amen.

92.  Do not chase the money, but chase the Most High God every day. Then, the money will chase you. Seek for Almighty God and His Kingdom, and everything you need, will come to you in its time. Amen.

93.  All the time remember that you are fully equipped, empowered, strengthened to overcome those obstacles that may come in your life. The Most High God already

gave you the strength, wisdom, sources, power and even the people to help you to solve your problems and difficulties you may (or would) face in your life. Almighty God gave you all these strengths and sources to win any problem, before the problem appeared in your path, and even before the creation of the World. Your Heavenly Father made you strong enough to win life problems. Amen. Remember those words.

94. Almighty God gave you the strengths to overcome the problems not only in your life, but also in the lives of the people surrounding you. You can live happily and, at the same time, you can help other people around you to be happy. You should never live, thinking only about yourself. We all need to help each other. That is how Our Heavenly Father wants us to live - helping and taking care of other people. Amen.

95. Don't give up during the tests you face in your life. You should continue fighting and moving forwards to your goals. How? By trusting Almighty God- Your Heavenly Father. The Most High God will make a way, when there is no way. God will bring the people to your life, when you need them. Never think of giving up on your dreams, God's Blessings, Wisdom and Promises for you and your family. That is how our Faith will be increased - Our Faith and Trust on the Most High God. Keep believing

and expecting the Huge Blessings, Gifts and Talents into your life and the lives of the people surrounding you.

96. The Most High God gives us problems, difficulties, problematic people, enemies, bad news, sicknesses in order to direct us and make us stronger, smarter and to test our Faith on God. The Most High God tests us, by giving us those obstacles in order to see, if we trust on Him and if we rely on Him. Will you give up and get upset, when you face a problem or difficulty in your life? Or will you continue moving towards your goals and dreams by trusting on God and by following all His principles? You have to make this choice. If you continue your life, trusting and relying on Almighty God, then the Most High God will take you to the places, you have never been before. God will give you the Blessings, you never dreamed about.

97. Almighty God gives us the problems to make us strong, smart and generous. With the help of the obstacles, the Most High God helps us to find out the talents, gifts and strengths that He gave us to succeed in this world. The problems in our lives will push us to become the difference makers in this world. If we discover those talents or a talent that Our Heavenly Father gave us, even before the creation of this world, then nothing can separate us from the Huge Blessings, which have our

name on them; the Blessings that will take us to the places, where we have not been before; the Blessings, which will make us happy, healthy and help us to reach our highest potentials. All the problems and difficulties that Almighty God gave us, as a result, will become the Blessings for our lives and for the people around us.

98. The things that the Most High God asks us to do are very simple. They are: to follow Him (the Creator of the Universe); rely on Him (on Almighty God); to trust on God, when there is no way out in a situation; to read the Bible as often as we can; to help the people as much as we can. Trust Almighty God by doing what God asks you to do, even when you do not want to do that. Do not be afraid to follow Our Heavenly Father and to trust Almighty God every time, and in every situation of your life. Remember that there is always a way for the Most High God to solve each your problem. The Most High God is never late in helping us. Our Job is to trust Our Heavenly Father and rely on Him, when we are facing the huge difficulties.

99. Keep the piece in your heart. Every time, remind yourself and the people around you the following words: "Everything will be ok. Everything will be perfect. Almighty God has the way out, when we do not have a way out. The Most High God is fighting our battles.

Almighty God is making our ways, putting the right people in the right places and the right chances for us. Almighty God is Our Provider and Vindicator."

100. Why do we expect the Blessings from Our Heavenly Father to be something small? Why? Why do we expect small Blessings from Almighty God? He created the Universe and everything in this world, and in the Heaven and Hell. Remember that.

101. Remember that the Most High God will never allow our enemies to bring any bad things or events into Our Lives, if only Almighty God has a Huge Plan to use those bad events for our success. The Most High God will use Our Problems, Mistakes, and All Negative things in Our Lives like the food steps to push us forward to our happiness and success.

102. When you have God's blessings in your life and you are happy, remind yourself about the days, when you had been in need. Never forget about those days, when you had the problems. Remind yourself how the Most High God helped you during those difficult days. During your happy days remember your sad, in need and unlucky days.

103. Remember that only Almighty God makes people successful, rich, in need or poor. It is God's choice to give us the life, happiness, prosperity, health; or the problem,

disease and loss in our lives. It is our job to accept everything from the Most High God with thankfulness. Accept from Almighty God both the happy days and sad days with thankfulness. Never stop praying. If you stop praying and appreciating God's blessings in your life during your happy days, then the Most High God will bring the problems and obstacles into your life to remind you about the importance of praying and spending time with Almighty God.

104. Do not loose your Fear of the Most High God. Be afraid of the Creator of the Universe and His anger every day of your life. The fear from Our Heavenly Father is the first thing that we need to have in order to be happy in this world.

105. When you need to make a decision in your life, first of all, listen to your heart. At the same time, pray and ask the Most High God to direct you to make the right decisions in every situation of your life.

106. Do not eat more than you need, because some of the diseases come from overeating of the food. Do not eat everything that you see and want to eat. Control your appetite.

107. Whatever you believe that God is asking you to do, please, do that to the best of your ability. Be a person that is determined to do, what the Most High God asked

you to do. Remember that Almighty God will never ask you to do something, if he does not give you the power and the ability to do that. His Grace is always sufficient.

108. Trust the Most High God in every second of your life and do the good things to the people surrounding you. Do as much good as you can to everybody that you can, and everywhere that you can, and as long as you possibly can. There is a huge power in just being good to the people. Especially, it gets more power, when you do something good for the people, who hurt you.

109. Live pleasing and serving the Most High God during your entire life. Every morning wake up and do what you believe would please Almighty God to the best of your ability. We need to live in order to please the Most High God. We need to show other people that we are children of the Most High God not only by our words, but also by our decisions, by our actions and by the way of our living, following God's words and by helping other people.

110. Do not be overcome by evil, but overcome evil with good - Romans 12:21 (Bible, New International Version). The way to overcome any evil that has been done to a person is to go out and do something good for somebody else. I believe this is one of the hidden secrets of Almighty God's Kingdom.

I believe that my book "My Visions from Almighty God" will prove the people, who are reading it the fact, which we need to read the Bible every day. We need to live according to God's words and principles that show us what is "good" and what is "wrong" (sin) in our world. With the help of my book, I want to underline the fact that if we want to reach a success in our lives; if we want to keep the perfect relationship with the Most High God; if we want to live by pleasing Almighty God – we need to follow God's words and we need to trust the Most High God in every difficult situation of our journey in this world.

We need to know that when we are in a trouble or when we meet the obstacles in our lives – the Most High God is telling us at that time: "Dear my child, help other people to solve their problems and I will help you to solve your problems". When I was in a trouble, the Most High God told those words inside of my heart. We have to live by helping the people around us. It is impossible to live happily by only thinking of our needs and us. Every day we need to try to be the "Blessing" for the people with whom we live and work, our relatives and our friends. Of course, we need to start that work from our homes and our families. The other important thing for us to do is to let the Most High God use our lives and us to show His Glory, Power, and Love to His children; and to save as many people as possible from going to Hell.

Today my Mom and my sister are reading the Bible. I am so

happy that Almighty God is changing my sister's and my Mom's hearts. The Most High God is improving my life and the lives of my relatives. I will continue praying and asking the Most High God to give my sister, my Mom, my brother and my father – His (God's) Wisdom. So, they will make decision to be baptized as soon as it is mentioned to be. All my relatives from my native country are very nice with my family and me today. Thanks to Almighty God for everything in my life.

I am very thankful to the Most High God for giving me the chance to share my "life events" with you and for helping me, in writing my book in order to show the readers "the Glory and the Power of the Creator of the Universe" through my life. Today, I understood that Almighty God gave me for a very good reason all the obstacles and the health problems that I had had during my life, so I would be able to show His Glory and Power, by writing the book about my life and sharing the knowledge that Almighty God gave me in my book "My Visions from Almighty God".

I want to say "Thank You" to Almighty God for helping me in writing this book about God's Glory and Victory in my life. I want to say "thank you" to all other people, who spent their time reading my book "My Visions from Almighty God". I want to ask an apology from my readers for the mistakes, which I may have in my book. I wish to every single person in our world to have the best life from Our Heavenly Father. *God Bless you all in every sphere of your life. In Jesus Name Amen.*

Printed in the United States
By Bookmasters